DAWN LIGHT

DAWN
LIGHT

~

Dancing with Cranes and
Other Ways to Start the Day

Diane Ackerman

W. W. NORTON & COMPANY
NEW YORK   LONDON

"Wake on Impermanence" by Eihei Dogen from *Zen Poems of China and Japan* translated and compiled by Lucien Stryk and Takashi Ikemoto. Copyright © 1973 by Lucien Stryk, Takashi Ikemoto, and Taigan Takayama. Used by permission of Grove/Atlantic, Inc.

"Haiku of Kobayashi Issa," translated by David G. Lanoue: http://haikuguy.com/issa.

Permission to reprint translation of Sappho poem granted by Martin West.

Excerpts from *The Pillow Book of Sei Shonagon*, translated and edited by Ivan Morris (1967). Copyright © 1991 Columbia University Press. Reprinted with permission of Columbia University Press and Oxford University Press.

Permission to reprint translations of Matsuo Basho haikus granted by Liza Dalby.

Rumi quote from *Open Secrets: Versions of Rumi*, edited by John Mayne and Coleman Barks © 1999. Reprinted by arrangement with Shambhala Publications Inc., Boston, MA. www. shambhala.com.

Haiku by George Swede from *Almost Unseen: Selected Haiku of George Swede*. Brooks Books, 2000.

For information about permission to reproduce selections from this book, write to Permissions, W. W. Norton & Company, Inc., 500 Fifth Avenue, New York, NY 10110

For information about special discounts for bulk purchases, please contact W. W. Norton Special Sales at specialsales@wwnorton.com or 800-233-4830

Manufacturing by Courier Westford
Book design by Ellen Cipriano
Production manager: Anna Oler

Library of Congress Cataloging-in-Publication Data

Ackerman, Diane, 1948–
Dawn Light : dancing with cranes and other ways to start the day / Diane Ackerman. — 1st ed.
    p. cm.
ISBN 978-0-393-06173-4 (hardcover)
1. Seasons—Psychological aspects. 2. Nature—Psychological aspects.
3. Human beings—Effect of environment on. 4. Meditations. 5. Satisfaction. I. Title.
QB637.2.A35 2009
508.2—dc22   2009023459

W. W. Norton & Company, Inc.
500 Fifth Avenue, New York, N.Y. 10110
www.wwnorton.com

W. W. Norton & Company Ltd.
Castle House, 75/76 Wells Street, London W1T 3QT

1 2 3 4 5 6 7 8 9 0

For my mother,
who always found time to marvel,
and who once described sunrise
in Kowloon Bay with such relish
that I can picture it even now

CONTENTS

AUTUMN

WINTER

This grand show is eternal. It is always sunrise
somewhere; the dew is never all dried at once;
a shower is forever falling; vapor is ever rising.
Eternal sunrise, eternal sunset, eternal dawn and
gloaming, on sea and continents and islands,
each in its turn, as the round earth rolls.

—JOHN MUIR

This world of ours—
To what shall I compare it?
To the white waves of a boat
That disappear without trace
As it rows away at dawn.

—SHAMI MANSEI,
EIGHTH CENTURY

A DAWNING PLEASURE

~

A T DAWN, THE WORLD RISES out of darkness, slowly, sense-grain by grain, as if from sleep. Life becomes visible once again. "When it is dark, it seems to me as if I were dying, and I can't think anymore," Claude Monet once lamented. "More light!" Goethe begged from his deathbed. Dawn is the wellspring of more light, the origin of our first to last days as we roll in space, over 6.684 billion of us in one global petri dish, shot through with sunlight, in our cells, in our minds, in our myriad metaphors of rebirth, in all the extensions to our senses that we create to enlighten our days and navigate our nights.

Thanks to electricity, night doesn't last as long now, nor is it as dark as it used to be, so it's hard to imagine the terror of our ancestors waiting for daybreak. On starless nights, one can feel like a loose array of limbs and purpose, and seem smaller, limited to what one can touch. In the dark, it's hard to tell friend from foe. Night-roaming predators may stalk us.

Reminded of all our delectable frailities, we become vulnerable as prey. What courage it must have taken our ancestors to lie down in darkness and become helpless, invisible, and delusional for eight hours. Graceful animals stole through the forest shadows by night, forbidding, distorted, maybe even ghoulish or magical. Small wonder we personalized the night with demons. Eventually, people were willing to sacrifice anything—wealth, power, even children—to ransom the sun, immense with life, a one-eyed god who fed their crops, led their travels, chased the demons from their dark, rekindled their lives.

Whatever else it is, dawn is always a rebirth, a fresh start, even if familiar routines and worries charge in clamoring for attention. While waking, we veer between dreamy and lucid (from the Latin *lux*, light). Crossing that threshold each morning, we step across worlds, half a mind turned inward, the other half growing aware. "I'm still a little *groggy*," we say, the eighteenth-century word for being drunk on rum. It's a time of epic uncertainty and vulnerability, as we surface from disorienting dreams and the blindness of keeping eyes shut for many hours. As the eyelids rise to flickering light and the dimly visible, it's easy to forget where we are, even what we are. Then everything shines. Paths grow easier to see, food easier to spot, jobs easier to tackle with renewed vigor. In rising light, doors and bridges become eye-catching. We may use all our other senses in the dark, but to see we need the sun spilling over the horizon, highlighting everything and pouring a thick yellow vitamin into our eyes. We're usually too hurried to savor the elemental in our lives: the reeling sun, moon, and stars; prophecy of clouds; ruckus of birdsong; moss brightly blooming; moon shadows and dew; omens of autumn in late summer; fizzy air before a storm; wind chime of leaves; fellowship of dawn and dusk. Yet we abide by forces so old we've lost the taste of their spell. It's as survivors that we greet each day.

When the sun fades in winter, we're instinctively driven to heights of craft and ingenuity. In the Northeast, rising humans slip from their quilted night-nests and keep warm in heat gusted by fires trapped in metal boxes. Sometimes they venture out wearing a medley of other life-forms: sap from rubber trees attached to the feet; soft belly hair from Mideastern goats wrapped around the head; pummeled cowskin fitted over the fingers; and, padding chest and torso, layers of long thickwalled plant cells humans find indigestible but insulating and plants use to buttress their delicate tissues—that is, galoshes, wool, leather gloves, and cotton underwear. Some humans go walking, jogging, or biking—to suck more oxygen from the air—which lubricates their joints, shovels fuel into their cells, and rouses their dozy senses. Some of us migrate south like elk or hummingbirds.

Right around Charleston, South Carolina, morning begins to change its mood, winter brings a chill but doesn't roll up your socks, and the sun boils over the horizon a moment sooner, because the planet swells a smidgeon there, just enough for pecan light at dawn, snapdragons and camellias too dewsodden to float scent, and birds tuning their pipes, right on schedule, for a chatterbox chorale.

By January, the northern bird chorus has flown to cucaracha-ville—or, if you prefer it anglicized, palmetto-bugville—where swarming insects and other lowlife feed flocks of avian visitors. There they join many of the upright apes they left behind: "snow birds" who also migrate to the land of broiling noons. We may travel far in winter, but our birds travel with us.

Painting its own time zone, its own climate, dawn is a land of petrified forests and sleeping beauties, when dry leaves, hardened by frozen dew, become ghost hands, and deer slouch through the woods, waiting for their food to defrost. Part of the great parentheses of our lives, dawn summons us to a world alive and death-defying, when the deepest arcades of life and matter beckon. Then, as if a lamp were switched on in a dark room, nature grows crisply visible, including our own nature, ghostly hands, and fine sediment of days.

DAWN MOTHER

~

WE SAY THE DAY DAWNS when the sun's leading edge
floats over the horizon, or when we wake, or when any
truth becomes known, or when the sky brightens enough to
dispel demons, vampires, trolls, and other light-hating villains.
Women used to be named "Dawn" as a charm to protect them
against evil. Mata Hari, the stage name of infamous Dutch
actress, courtesan, and spy Margaretha Geertruida Zelle (1876–
1917), means "the eye of the day" (from the Malay *mata*, "eye,"
and *hari*, "dawn, day"). English for day's eye is daisy, the flower
whose petals open at dawn and close at twilight. But many
nuances of dawn lighten our world.

The dawn that banishes evil spirits is *astronomical dawn*,
well before sunrise when, technically, the sun dangles 18
degrees below the horizon. Then comes *nautical dawn*, when
the horizon and some objects become visible but the sun still
hangs 12 degrees below the horizon. In *civil dawn*, the final
hour before sunrise, the sun rides only 6 degrees below the

horizon, high enough to clarify objects, emblazon the sky with light, and allow work to begin. And there's the farmer's friend, *rooster dawn*. The ancient Romans divided the day into sixteen pieces of one and a half hours each beginning at midnight. Roosters crowed in the third watch, the *diliculum*, or morning twilight, which gives us our word *dawn*.

Most languages honor dawn with one short word. But in ancient Japan, the day was divided into twelve two-hour watches, each named after a zodiacal sign, further segmented into quarters. The months were classified by signal natural events: Rice-sprouting Month, Watery Month, Frost Month, etc. And the "year-periods" were labeled by the Japanese government. So, to specify dawn (6:00 a.m.) on February 15, A.D. 998, I would have to write: "The fourth quarter of the watch of the Tiger on the fifteenth day of the Sprouting Month in the fourth year of the Chotoku year-period, in which the Elder Brother of the Earth coincided with the sign of the Dog."

All dawns delight me. No two people experience the same dawn, psychologically or literally. On the equator, dawn unfolds in minutes; at the poles it can stretch for hours. Only as dawn's final drama does the sun actually rise. We say "rise" with typical human self-centeredness, as if we could bend even a third-magnitude star to our will. Rolling from west to east, the earth keeps tilting different faces to the sun, which *appears* to rise. "Night falls," we say, as if it were the closing curtain in a one-act play. But, really, day falls—we fall toward and roll away from the sun. As we do, the cold shadow we call night rises all around us and the star-baked earth begins to lose its warmth, until dawn, when we face the sun's hot breath once more.

On clear days, I look up at the edgeless blue and follow it in my mind's eye to where sky becomes outer space. Then

I say silently, always with reverent surprise, as if it had just occurred to me for the first time: *We live on a planet, a planet in space, surrounded by millions of other planets and suns. And on this planet, eons ago, by chance life evolved.* Then I picture the cavalcade of life, from grub-like strings of bacteria and knobs of blue-green algae through weird mammals to people, in suits and shoes, driving metal shells, talking into electronic ears, having dinner dates, creating art, craving love, living in palatial huts.

How strange and eye-poppingly wonderful it is to live on a planet in space, and to be alive with intelligence, maybe something unique thus far in our relatively young universe. I'm often startled by this thought, like the way you flinch when someone surprises you. How unlikely, and what an *adventure.* For me, it's important to wake up often to our true nature and circumstance, to remember how lucky and fleeting it is *just being alive.* Most often that happens outside, while walking or biking in the country, or enjoying a park in the manicured wilderness of a city.

Being in nature at dawn always comforts me. I say that as a sort of shorthand, because it's really a mental knot. I do find it comforting to be in nature. But how can you be *in* what you *are?* All of our being, juices, flesh, and spirit occurs as nature; nature surrounds, permeates, effervesces in, and includes us. At the end of our days it deranges and disassembles us like old toys banished to the basement. There, once living beings, we return to our non-living elements, but still and forever remain a part of nature.

Maybe using the word "wilderness" would feel truer than "nature." Like circus lions, we'll always be wild and fiercely unpredictable. We build more curious habitats than other animals, who, to the best of my knowledge, don't require anything like electric cow-milk frothing machines, beeswax on a flaming string, or vaporized flower essence mixed with musk from the anal sac of civets, to encourage breeding. But I could be wrong. Maybe the wren's adagio is equally extravagant. And I'm reluctant to hazard a guess about the necking and petting of alligators, whose cheeks are studded with exquisitely sensitive pleasure nodes. Even at our most domesticated and tame, we're like pet zebras or grizzly bears, dangerous to anger, always flirting with a tantrum just under the well-behaved surface.

For me, nature means the full wallet of Creation, which sometimes requires a little quantum thinking if I want to include the earliest stages of the universe. I see, in my mental picture frame, a tough silky ball of hydrogen floating in an endless ether. Then parallel universes that collided and mamboed apart. Nature includes both the one and the many, the squirmingly minute and the invisibly huge.

The word *naturally* has at least two meanings in most languages. First, and originally, the ways of the natural world, as in the naturally changing seasons because Earth circles the Sun. And then there's the "but of course, it stands to reason" *naturally* used to emphasize what goes without saying, and then saying it anyway. Just as dawn follows night, it implies, what I'm going to say is inevitable, an agreed-upon truth indisputable as the Alps. The words *nature* and *naturally* come from the Latin *natura* (the dawn, character, and drama of life), which stems from an even older word, *nasci*, "to be born" from an ancient mother.

In 2000, Chinese scientists unearthed a 125-million-year-old fossil of a rodent-like creature they named *Eomaia scansoria*, "dawn mother." Whenever we call someone a *rat* we're really harking back to our earliest ancestors, tiny tree-hugging placental rodents that fled from the feet and teeth of dinosaurs by scurrying up any available tree. After the dinosaurs died out, dawn mothers could safely emerge, and they thrived, in time turning into all sorts of species. We descended from those tree shrews—five-inch-long mousy little beings that weighed under a pound, used hardy claws to climb, ate insects, and were all fur and appetite. They were the first creatures to nourish a baby inside the mother's body, the first mammal of the sort that populates the earth today with elephants and wombats and weasels and humans. Let others appeal to Aurora, Eos, and other goddesses when they wake. I prefer to thank the small, timid dawn mother in us all.

SPRING

~

PALM BEACH, FLORIDA

DAWN AMONG THE PALMS

⌒

THE SKY IS FLORIDIAN MYTHIC: a dazzling sun-gloss blue over ocean and palm trees. Cloud plumes rise like smoke on the horizon. But farther inland, fat heavy clouds line up in parallel, with bottoms so flat they look underlined. In this magical haze, a flock of flamingos pinking by would not seem odd. Instead a lone boat-tailed grackle glides steeply to the roof of a white stucco building where parked cars roost.

This is not a typical spring day in my hometown in upstate New York, ruled by red-winged blackbirds, lilacs, apple trees, and snowmelt. That both realities can exist at the same time, a thousand miles apart, continues to amaze me. The mind contains a million snow globes, shakes this one or that, and watches sand or snow fall in slow motion through the gels of memory.

As the sun seeps over the horizon, people crossing the street create shadows twice their body length, and it's a little odd to see their upright bodies trailing perpendicular shadows.

All is surface brilliance, the edges and faces shine, the shadows are slightly elongated and narrow. Is this what sculptor Alberto Giacometti saw, I wonder, the shadows we unknowingly drag along the ground behind us like tails we tend not to see?

When the sun strikes the dewy leaves of most any plant, frond, or bush, they spangle, and soon the chrome car bumpers splatter light like stars. The sun has crystallized the colored carapaces humans use for travel, armor, and display. Just because we didn't evolve the beetle's shell or the armadillo's plates doesn't mean we can't fabricate our own. The clouds lose their oatmeal heaviness and lie still, puddled in light. At last the sun rises high enough that I feel its warm breath on my face, a soft dry heat as mind and day dawn.

With a noise between a whinny and a dying train whistle, a collared dove pops into view ten inches in front of my nose, tail flared wide, wings furiously back-flapping. Moments before, I was calmly watching the sea, where a pink and gray sunrise echoed the cheap linoleum in 1950s motels. The uprising dove didn't see me lying on a chaise beside the white balustrade, *its* balustrade, not my balcony rail.

Presto chango, it stalls and turns in midair while fixing me with one glossy black eye. A shiny eye, despite the early hour. *Mar, mar, mar,* it complains as it settles on a railing only a yard away. Then it swaggers to the next balcony, and launches itself up to the Moorish roof where domed terracotta tiles make perfect dovecotes.

The dove descending breaks the air / With flame of incandescent terror, T. S. Eliot writes in *The Four Quartets.* This one doesn't seem alarmed by our encounter; collared doves tolerate humans. With the climate changing and garden birds winging farther south to find new niches, doves have begun paying regular house calls. Frequent visitors, they seem to enjoy city life *among* humans, we endless purveyors of garbage and other handouts, as much as humans do.

Partly folding their wings to lose altitude, they look like experimental jets darting down to land, and they're heavy enough to pick up real speed. The landing itself is usually a controlled stall, with tail feathers spread like a Sioux head-dress beneath them and wings rapidly beating. I like to watch doves throttle their flutter speed—from a polite fanning (think gloved women in drawing rooms) to frantic dippy correctives. Their relatives, the mourning doves, zigzag more and sometimes whistle as they fly, but also like to camp out with humans. To enough of us, the informal naming committee, their *oh-woo-woo-woo* sounds like the melancholy lament of pallbearers, and so we condemn them to endless mourning.

Two flocks of collared doves roller-coaster through the air, each bird distinct as they flap to a high point, then suddenly turn with a flash of pale bellies and rocket down the sky, careening around a sharp invisible bend to zoom up the sky again for another rush downhill. Over and over the two flocks ply the winds, often crossing in midair, then shuffling like a deck of cards, only to fly apart perfectly unscathed into their fugitive mobs. How do they avoid each other at such speed while being carried along by high winds? I've never seen any collide and fall. Surely these calisthenics, scary as they must be at times, rouse them from stupor, get their blood flowing, and test their mettle. Which bird leads? Are stragglers noticed and judged?

Although their mass intuition to wheel and turn appears almost telepathic, it's *emergent* behavior—a term sometimes used to describe consciousness in humans—a knowing that materializes when individuals (doves, cells, bees, neurons) unwittingly work in unison. The tiny ghost ants that flit across Floridian floors don't require a plan to forage, build nests, create a bustling colony. Following pheromone footprints and counting their steps, each ant need only stumble upon a few cooperative neighbors. From that random mix a rambunctious organism can emerge with its own distinctive caste system and behaviors. If it prospers, it thrives. So, too, the myriad cells in a human brain, any one of which is witless. Mind results solely from the *relation* of the parts to the whole, the genius of the swarm. Nature promotes the crowd of individuals, the one among the many, the single doves and the wheeling flock that moves as one enterprise.

With gray-pink head and wings the color of wet sand, the adults sport a thin black and white band around the back of the neck. *U-nite-id*, they coo while roosting, and sometimes *I don't know*. When they fly, they stop singing and cry out a nasal *kwurr kwurr!*

I'm not sure why the doves settle, take wing a few minutes later, settle, fly like a single knife blade icing the sky, settle again, fly again. Maybe they circle and perch until most are content with their neighbors. When only a few gather, they sit a body-width apart, which seems to be the personal space they prefer. If crowded, they bunch tight as straphangers on a subway and they squabble more.

Can there really be no leader? Watching each morning, I haven't detected one. When they lift off and fly suddenly, they always appear galvanized but startled, whipped up by some other bird's whim. More chaos theory than marching orders. Other animals herd, school, cluster, huddle, crowd, swarm to gain safety in numbers, with a hundred eyes scouting instead of two (eight in the case of migrating tarantulas). The laggards fly at risk and are easier to pick off. Veering and whirling with apparent randomness, the flock becomes too erratic to predict. A hawk, owl, or other predator won't focus on any one dove and risk plunging into a mass of beaks. Flocking is far safer, makes navigation easier, and food and nest areas quicker to find.

In a 1984 issue of *Nature*, Wayne Potts published his research on sandpipers which he filmed and then studied frame by frame. Any bird could rally the flock with a slight movement that spread quickly as a "maneuver wave." He found that birds only followed other birds banking *into* the flock, not away from it, because leaving the flock was dangerous. A simple rule, it protects individuals from being nabbed by predators, but also from having to make many decisions.

What's wondrous and strange is that when a maneuver wave begins it moves through the flock faster than the reaction time of any one bird. In his lab, Potts tested a bird's reaction time to a light flash: 38 milliseconds. Yet maneuver waves spread at less than 15 milliseconds. Not for all the birds. The first to follow suit usually takes about 67 milliseconds. Potts speculates that the birds farthest away from the "initiator" see the wave coming and get ready to react, an instinct he calls the "chorus-line hypothesis," after the Radio City Rockettes and other lines of synchronized high-kicking dancers. Films of chorus lines support his hypothesis. If one dancer suddenly begins a high kick, the others react one after the other at intervals of 108 milliseconds, even though the visual reaction time of humans is 194 milliseconds. Although we're the most social animal on the planet, we rarely speak of our own conjoined intelligence, how often we operate as flocks, yearn-ing to "fit in." We say, and really mean: "Let's put our heads together." Too easily, perhaps, we follow the crowd, join cults and congregations, adopt the path and view of the herd. We form committees, charities, militias, political parties, think tanks, symposia, juries—like doves, we eagerly become part of one biological cadence.

Even on windless days, doves flock and swoop, veering aimlessly over parking lots and sunlit terracotta walls, tourists and locals. Any movement by one bird, however random, can press the flock to change direction, speed, or altitude. Based on simple rules, their actions and reactions result in winged complexity. In 1986, computer wizard Craig Reynolds created what he called "boids," perfect flocking organisms that inhabit only computers. By studying them, Reynolds arrived at three rules they follow: (1) *separation*—steer to avoid flock mates; (2) *alignment*—adopt the heading of flock mates; and (3) *cohesion*—stay close to flock mates. Computer-generated flocks of bats and penguins based on boids were first used in the film *Batman Returns* in 1992, and have appeared in many other films since then. And, based on flocking algorithms, the British firm Swarm Systems will soon market an UltraSwarm, a flying cluster of computerized "Owls" that can fly and work together without colliding. The U.S. military is particularly interested in these packs of swarming robots that know how to cooperate, some small as wrens or dragonflies, others creeping spiderlike to scout inside buildings.

Not boids, but real collared doves arrive from several directions, turn loosely above the crowded wires and settle, unsettling others who take wing, loop around the neighborhood, and return. They are restless this morning, and grab the wires for only a moment or two, then arise like a shake of pepper, scatter, split into separate cohorts, reassemble shoulder to shoulder, take flight again with the sun bouncing off their white belly feathers each time they turn in unison. Does the sun feel hot on their bellies? I think so. Rain-soaked birds often stand with wings outstretched, drying in the sun.

The doves perch and reassemble faster than I can track their whims in ink. Now they are evenly spaced, like black rivets, against the cloud-mottled sky. I wonder if they can feel our vocal vibrations humming in their feet. With the sound of someone casually opening a paper bag, the doves lift up all at once from the telephone wires. Undulating, they edge into and out of sight, sweeping palm-flat overhead, as they skid slantwise across the sky, with some fliers dropping out of existence into a pocket of fog, only to reappear magically elsewhere. Once more they settle on the wires.

My mind's binocular lens swoops straight to one particular dove, whose wing flapping I imagine in my own wing muscles, whose feathers lifted by the cool breeze lift my windblown hair. Sound churns in my chest and burbles up my throat automatically. I recognize my neighbors beside me on the telephone wire, do not feel threatened by them, do not touch them unless the breeze blows just hard enough to unsettle me and then my wings spring back, up, and flap, my feet release, and I touch feathers on both sides as I settle, unsettling them. I feel the sun baking my feathers, the faint telephone wire hum in my feet, the mindless upflapping, banking, and planing.

I remember skidding airplanes across the sky like that, on purpose, to lose altitude on final. Oh, but what clumsy and rigid wings humans use, so limited in the subtle flexions of bird flight. In birds, feather windows open on upbeats, close on downbeats; they feel the air breathing through their wings.

In airplanes, we open stiff heavy doors on our extended wings (pilots call the doors *flaps*), and let air slip between plates of metal.

At 7:00 a.m. the humans emerge in vehicles and on foot, while great flocks of doves dance and swoop above them, and cars pass with the sound of breaking waves. A yellow cab arrives and a young man in blue jeans and orange shirt tosses a suitcase and a carry-on into the trunk, slams metal on metal, squeaks the back door open, and climbs in, slamming the door after him, as he sets off to join the rest of his flock. Only ten minutes later, a brightness indivisible from the idea of day settles, illuminating everything.

JUST A LITTLE RAIN

～

A FULL MOON IS BLAZING IN a rain-cleansed sky, an atmospheric stunner for which the Japanese have a specific word. In Japanese, many words are built around the basic kanji for rain, 雨, a drawing that evokes raindrops blowing slantwise across a decorative door or screen. In addition to all the usual water words familiar in English (snow, hail, sleet, fog, rain date, cloudburst, etc.), the Japanese have seventeen words based on rain that have to do with tears, mortality, flimsiness, and dew, and a catalog of specific terms for rain and how we perceive and behave in rain, including: waiting for a break in the rain, early-summer rain, moon shining in a rain-cleansed sky, a stretch of sunshine after the rain, rain that keeps people indoors, struggling through wind and rain, bamboo shoots after a rain, canceled only in case of heavy rain, welcome rain during a drought, rain shower during a dust storm, first rain to fall between late autumn and early winter, preparing for rain, polluted rain, refreshing rain that falls once every ten days, being unable to see the harvest moon because of rain, and my personal favorite—a man or woman whose presence seems to cause rain. As though enacting those last two, there's a televison soap opera in Colombia called *La Tormenta* (The Thunderstorm), which retails the love lives of men and women whose very presence does indeed seem to incite storms.

That English has a cornucopia of rain words and terms is fortunate, because just as flavor is equal parts taste and smell, rain is as much feel as sight, and also has a scent. We distinguish easily between drizzle, virga (rain that doesn't touch the ground), and downpour, *a real toad-strangler*. The scent of spring rain bounces up off the fertile ground and down from the budding trees. Texans describe rain pelting slantwise: *like a cow pissing sideways onto a rock.*

But we haven't a word for the eerie rain at dawn that falls out of a slate-gray sky, or invisible night rain, or the transparent sheets of rain that blow under a streetlamp, or the ropy rain that flails at odd moments, or the pockets of light rain that fall as single clouds pass over a backyard, or the gelatinous rain that builds just before sleet, or the blue drapes of rain seen in the distance, or the shower that blows up at teatime every afternoon on some Caribbean islands, or the sandy rain that skirls along a beach, or the rain that literally falls once in a blue moon, or the perfectly domed raindrops clinging to glass, or rain pitting your face as you sprint through it, or loud vibrating rain that charges down pipes and gutters, or the sound of rain hitting leaves, or the rivulets of rain meandering down windowpanes, or the tinny rain that drums on the roof of a car, or the rhythmic rain that one mistakes for approaching footsteps, or the rain that falls thick as rubber in the Amazon.

To name only a few of the thousand nameless rains we know by sight and feel.

In Ireland, there's a saying that the only way to tell the difference between winter and summer is to measure the temperature of the rain. The Irish take great sonorous delight in calling their rains by name, including: *biadhan tsic*, rain in frosty weather; *cith agus dealán*, sunshine with showers; *ceóbhrán*, pale drizzle; *mist durach mor*, long shower; *fuarbháisteach earraigh*, a cold spring downpour; *greadadh báistí*, a pelting rain; *ceatha*, the breeze before a shower; *shíobhta bháistí*, a continuous, driving rainstorm; and *taom fearthainne*, a total sky-opening bucketing down of rain.

Hawaiians require over a hundred names for rain, including *kolele ua*, a light moving rain; *`olulo*, a storm beginning out at sea; and *kahiko o ke akua*, rain that's so beautiful it must be the adornment of the gods. Since it rains most of the time in some parts of Hawaii, the rainbow, *anuenue*, abounds, and even the University of Hawaii's sports teams are named the Rainbows. Some languages, like German, contain words designed to capture the sound of rain: *pladdern* (heavy rain with big drops), *prasseln* (heavy rain but smaller drops), *giessen* (pouring rain), *sprühen* (spray-like rain), *tropfern* (dripping).

In China, flowering apricot rain only falls during the winter, when nearly all the landscape is withered, but drifts of apricot trees bloom like living snow. One yellow-blossomed tree, planted 1,600 years ago during the Jin dynasty, still continues to flower. Tall trees that bloom amid desolation, they symbolize resilience and evoke cranes. A slender, pretty woman hurrying through the rain may be said to have "a crane's body, and flowering apricot tree's bones."

Some sleep-noise gizmos include the sound of light rain, a soft hypnotic purr that most people find soothing. But no rain is ever peaceful, since raindrops are changing shape violently as they fall, colliding with dust and one another, pulsing at 300 times per second through a tirade of forms: domed, flat-bottomed, elongated, egg, fat, skinny, flat, pill-like, tall. Even the gentlest rain is a sea of furious crack-ups and mutations. Similarly, we appear to be whole, even serene in our abundantly calm moments, but like the shape of rain, we are a deluge of small processes, interactions, and relations, changing by the nanosecond, yet somehow holding a fragile sense of self intact.

A CALAMITY OF CRANES

The world? Moonlit
drops shaken
from the crane's bill.

—EIHEI DOGEN,
THIRTEENTH CENTURY

SOON AFTER SUNRISE, A SILHOUETTE glides above the
water, huge wings outstretched, long neck straight as a
compass needle, legs trailing behind. Pelican? Snow goose?
Tundra swan? Possibly a pelican this far south, but those long
trailing legs give me pause, and suddenly the rarity registers in
my psyche. The long legs and neck don't belong to pelicans.
I wonder if it could be a lone whooping crane gliding back to
its wintering grounds in south-central Florida. Cranes come
naturally to mind because this is the season of a great crane
pilgrimage.

It is said that Audubon once killed seven whooping cranes
with a single buckshot blast. In the 1940s only 15 whooping
cranes survived in all of America, and their future seemed

grim; by the 1990s, the wild flock had grown to only 133. Moved by their plight, Joe Duff and Bill Lishman, two artists turned biologists, founded Operation Migration in 1994. Lishman was already the first human to fly with birds, leading a gaggle of Canada geese with an ultralight (little more than a deck chair with a lawnmower engine) in local flights around Ontario in 1988.

Near extinction, animals can lose subtle parts of their culture critical for survival. Whoopers aren't colonial birds; it's not natural for them to flock. In the wild, they would learn to navigate the flyways from their parents—with *See one, do one, teach one* the unstated motto. Without that tutelage, a juvenile won't migrate, but try to brave out the harsh Midwestern winter instead. How do you teach migration to captive, orphan birds you've hatched from eggs? Only by hoodwinking them and posing as seasoned ultralight parents they can imprint on from birth, featherless knights in crane colors.

In the wild, a whooping crane will take off in midmorning and hitch a ride on a suite of thermals, perfectly balanced and attuned to the compound marvel of wind and feathers. It needn't land, or even flap much, at times rising as high as 6,000 feet, then gradually descending only to rise once more. Soaring for an hour on brisk winds, a crane flaps its wings less than a sparrow crossing a street. How can an ultralight compete? "These birds learn to fly off the wake created by the aircraft," Duff explains. "But that only works when the air is calm and the ultralight is steady." As a result, first light is always the departure hour.

When the birds returned on their own the following spring, Duff and Lishman continued flights—first with Canada geese, then non-endangered sandhill cranes, and finally with whooping cranes. Since then, Operation Migration aviculturists and workers at the USGS Patuxent Wildlife Research Center have been nestling crane eggs in incubators, turning them three times a day as their parents would in the wild, and serenading them—with recordings of a whooper parent's brood calls, natural sounds of the wetlands, and ultralight motors. After baking beneath heat lamps for twenty-nine to thirty days, they hatch. Then the workers don shapeless white robes (lest the birds learn to trust humans), feed them using a life-size, crane-headed handpuppet, and help the fledglings master the fluent migration of wild cranes. Only a week old, they learn to follow a taxiing ultralight, while whooper contact calls issue from the craft and the berobed pilot feeds them mealworms from the crane-headed puppet. During the long months of conditioning they ideally see no humans at all, only other cranes and a tribe of helpful baggy-robed ghosts.

Whooping cranes quickly endear themselves to people. A majestic five feet tall, adults are glacier-white birds with black-tipped wings, black mask, and red crown. Eyes are amber, bills tan, legs and toes black. Using a wingspan of seven feet, they famously dance a combination of bows, hops, leapfroggings, flapping, running, and stick or grass tossing, in what looks like a cross between a fan dance and a fandango. They dance during courtship and to fortify a pair bond, but also whenever the mood strikes them, if bored or just for fun. Even the juveniles dance, though in different attire, a plumage of white mottled with cinnamon-brown. I wonder what they make of their human mimics, such as the crane dancers among the Ostiaks of Siberia and the BaTwa of southern Africa, in ancient Turkey and even in mythic Greece, where Theseus supposedly performed a ritual crane dance after killing the Minotaur.

Like humans, cranes stand upright and walk on two legs; they form lifelong attachments sometimes compared to marriage, and mates stay together year-round; they rear young that remain juvenile for a long time. In captive breeding programs (as opposed to Operation Migration's work in the wild), cranes grow to recognize individual humans, treating each person differently, depending on their history with the person. "In fact, cranes that treat me with a good measure of circumspection," biologist Scott Swengel reveals, "may, in contrast, try to take advantage of new interns and attack them." Male and female cranes look much the same to us, but whooping cranes pay attention to human gender. "Male cranes are 'nicer' to our women employees than to men," Swengel adds, "while female cranes are nicer to men." Even as chicks, they prefer to follow humans of the opposite sex. And Swengel has noticed that some female cranes respond differently toward him if he's alone or with another person they like or dislike. They "become especially catty if the woman with me is someone with whom I have a significant emotional attachment, like my wife." Such human parallels make the cranes all the more appealing to their passionate protectors, and fill work days with a steady stream of trans-species intrigues. I don't believe these whooping cranes think as a thinker thinks, but they do problem-solve, experience an ensemble of feelings (including fidelity), play, hold grudges, recognize human faces even if hairstyle or clothes change, and many other tricks we regard as solely human. They can anticipate another animal's moves so they must be able to picture themselves in its place, faced with its needs and frights.

Dressed in white robes and hoods, wearing a whooping crane puppet head at the end of one sleeve, Operation Migration's wild-crane handlers appear to belong to an arcane religious church: the Order of Refined Destiny, or perhaps the Celebrants of the Crane. Beneath their robes they carry tape recorders that play crane sounds, and together they amble into the fields to forage and frolic. Just as crane parents would, they swim the chicks, for exercise and to strengthen the birds' legs for life in the wetlands, where they'll eat crabs, clams, frogs, and plants.

Finally, they teach the cranes to take flight together at dawn, flock and form chevrons across the sky, with the hardiest, most aggressive birds in front, spinning waves of air, and weaker or lower-ranking ones riding the surf, allowing all to travel at the same speed behind an ultralight acting as surrogate parent. As the most dominant bird, the non-flapping craft determines direction and when and where to land. Despite the young cranes' excitement, they learn to map the flyway to their winter home in the marshes of south-central Florida, where food abounds.

During the first five years, sixty chicks were taught the best thoroughfare from Wisconsin to Florida, flying at dawn because, like eagles and albatrosses, cranes soar with colossal fringed wings, hitching rides on thermals, columns of warm rising air. Do they sense the warmer air first on their wingtips, and turning into the warmth, enter an elevator heaving them higher and higher? Rising, do they feel the cool edge of a thermal and keep banking into its tower of lift? Does the free ride or the novelty entice them? As they grow, they learn where to find these invisible magic carpets.

I remember discovering this in a small high-winged airplane at noon on a broiling day over the Arizona desert, feeling the sudden boost under my wings whenever I entered a thermal, concerned about the sudden rush of altitude at first, and then banking into it, just for fun. Soon I scouted the sky for birds of prey on other thermals, noting that thermals form easily over hot flatlands. Little of this knowing would be unintelligible to a crane, which feels each twitch of a feather with a delicacy and detail it's hard for us to imagine. Suppose we could feel every hair on our arms?

Does the air taste different as a crane migrates, is that part of the sensory map it learns? Does it ford distinctive rivers of air, its own great Shenendoahs? I think so. Storks migrating from northern Europe to the Mediterranean and down to Africa follow the landmarks of rivers, towns, and lakes, committing them all to memory. They guide by the sun, moon, and stars, an inner magnetic compass, and other clues like a cavalcade of smells. These cranes, shown the route only once, stitch together a sensory map, which they can also read in reverse. No one has to show them how to fly home at season's end, above a world storied with scientists, well-wishers, and ardent fans, hoping for a rare glimpse of a bird that nests in the imagination of millions.

Cranes decorate the lives of many cultures, but in Oriental art, especially, cranes symbolize wisdom, eternal youth, and marital happiness, as in this haiku by eighteenth-century poet Kobayashi Yataro, who went by the name of Issa:

> In spring mist
> three pines, two cranes
> husband and wife

Traditionally, the bonsai-like art of haiku invokes a season and loads simple words with symbolism. So, to the readers of this haiku, both long-lived pines and monogamous cranes embody a happy marriage.

Flashing white wings and bellies, trailing long elegant legs, cranes soar above the noise and sorrow of the world, the only pure things among impure beings, rising with slow stately wing-beats. Cranes are often shown winging souls to heaven or ferrying sage recluses who use them as messengers. People embroider cranes on bridal kimonos. In folktales cranes can shape-shift and become maidens, and it's said that folding a thousand origami cranes will grant any wish or restore health. In the Himalayan kingdom of Bhutan, cranes are honored as reincarnated beings pausing on earth to help others reach enlightenment. They're always depicted as stately, well-mannered gentlemen, incorruptible and naturally clean and honest.

In Greek and English legend, cranes warred with pygmy tribes and humans. At night, the crane acting as sentry would stand on one leg, clutching a large stone in the other. To signal danger, all it had to do was drop the stone, whose clatter would wake the sleeping army. If that sentry bird was surprised and killed, the stone would also fall, sounding the alarm of one stone clanking onto others. No one doubted that the stone's clattering would hammer through dreams, or that the sentry crane could stand on one leg with the other holding the stone aloft for hours. Therefore cranes often appeared in heraldry on coats of arms. After that, a branch of a family tree came to be called *pied de grue*, "foot of the crane,' which in time became the more succinct *pedigree*. A bird became an emblem, then a synecdoche (its foot implying the whole bird), which stood for a lineage, which entered the language as a symbol, the single word *pedigree*, which in the beginning conjured up its origin in the days of warring pygmies and cranes. Now the term has lost that resonance and struck out on its own, minus its colorful pedigree.

Today only 530 whooping cranes exist, 380 of them in the wild, and not all cranes migrate to Florida; some cohorts wing south to Texas from Canada. They're not known to grace New York with unexpected visitors. A neighbor phoned up excitedly one day, hoping she had a whooping crane (more likely a sandhill) strutting across her yard in Ithaca, browsing for a spell, much to the shock of her two house cats, then levitating on huge wings.

A friend's phone call brings the news: the cranes arrived safely at Chassahowitzka National Wildlife Refuge last night, just ahead of a violent thunderstorm. But horror followed. This morning, all but one were found dead, stunned by lightning and drowned. *Don't picture the individual cranes, legs twisted at grisly angles, lying dead in the marshes,* I counsel myself. But it is too late—the words gouge images in my mind and I am creased by sorrow. Duff describes the loss as "traumatic" for the handlers, and I'm not surprised. Their home flock had grown to 81 birds, and each class escorted south to learn the route had successfully migrated north in the spring and south again in the fall on their own.

"Our hearts are aching for the young birds that were lost," the team posts on the Operation Migration website. "These chicks were like our children; the start of a new generation of life for the species."

I mourn the lost cranes. *Lost,* we say, as in *lost at sea,* as if they've simply gone missing or strayed off course. When we talk about what's lost, we may think we all mean the same thing, but there are many permutations and subtleties of loss in nature, from the gradual clouding of view that frosts up a window in midwinter to the extinct flocks of passenger pigeons that once darkened the Midwestern sky. There are recoverable losses (the American eagle was only recently brought back from the brink) and ones irretrievable as the dodo, imminent losses like the Florida panther, upland gorilla, or Hawaiian monk seal, and losses incomprehensible as nineteenth-century milliners nearly obliterating the world's whooping cranes.

The lost cranes join a list that forms automatically in my mind, where many calibers of loss are stored: things once here but now gone, things in the process of vanishing, things that have mutated, things that exist but are unrecognizable, mythic things which never existed, people or animals who have died, bygone periods of one's life. All rankle, and yet a sense of loss and forgetting unifies my life, and so do the many things that surprise me by being resistant to loss, such as a college friendship renewing itself and thriving thirty years later, while others may gently decay like old driftwood.

Some losses are fully replaceable—wolves can be reintroduced into a national park. Whooping cranes can be hand-reared and taught how to migrate. Others allow only facsimiles—family groups of gorillas replaced by extended zoo-families. There are some conversations with nature we can no longer have, and I feel poorer without them. Imagine if woolly mammoths still roamed the steppes, if Neanderthals still raised their young on the savannas, if the botanical Edens of the early planet survived. Without them, how full is our sense of life on Earth?

THE LOST NIGHT SKY

TㅌHE BLACK SLATE OF NIGHT is chalked over with stars. Like a yellow firefly, Saturn hovers a knuckle's length above the thick crescent of Venus, while nearby the constellation Leo roars into view. Dawn is the best time to spot meteors, when the leading edge of our planet races right into a cloud of space dust and debris—like bugs splattering on the windshield of a speeding car. A meteor shower peaked last night, and I'm still seeing a dozen or so tears an hour. Twice that many should be visible, but light pollution veils the heavens.

In large cities, where the constellations are all on the ground and those in the sky rarely visible, some people belong to the "Dark Sky Society," a grassroots organization devoted to restoring the grandeur of star-loaded night skies by dimming unnecessary city and stadium lights and having a curfew on advertising signs. With the constellations hugging the ground and the sky veiled by light pollution, it's easy to lose one's sense of place. I live in a village adjoining a small city, and to find sky dark enough for a stirring view of prominent comets, we drive into the farmlands ten miles from town.

All these lights on the ground appear to be jumbling our circadian rhythms and health. When scientists used satellite photographs to measure the amount of night light in 147 cities, then overlaid them onto a map of breast cancer cases, they discovered that women living in the aura of the brightest streetlights were more likely to get breast cancer than those lit mainly by the moon and stars. A recent study indicates that women working under artificial light during night shifts suffer a 50 percent increase in cancer rates. Last year, as a result, the World Health Organization labeled night-shift work a carcinogen.

Still, streetlamps shine all night like pocket suns. Cinemas and groceries wear crowns of fluorescent light. What must the birds think? Do they adapt to our inverted ways, guided by all our electric stars and neon auroras? How have we come to create our own tame stars to guide us through our days? Our constellations are easier to control, our pots of cold fire more portable. Diurnal from birth, we weave these trails of false sunlight through the dangerous night world where our senses falter.

Sunlight is so important to us that even though it does exist, we had to invent it anyway, over and over, in lamps and torches of endless variety. Artificial rhythms and cycles may be efficient, and electric lighting a minor miracle, but they don't mesh well with old circadian rhythms, so we end up sleep-deprived and often depressed in winter. We Northerners mainly work or play indoors, by lamplight at night, and strangely enough, also by lamplight during the day, because most buildings, to conserve heat, haven't many windows.

Windows or not, there's little light to behold during the long winter known as *Mørketida* ("murky time"), the sunless months north of the Arctic Circle. On Tromsø, a hilly island nine hundred miles north of Oslo, Norway, the winter temperatures stay relatively balmy (17 to 30 degrees Fahrenheit), thanks to the Gulf Stream, and there's no permafrost, no tundra. But by mid-December, without a visible sun, dawn and dusk merge, and only a gray sky and purple horizon signal noon. According to Tromsø psychiatrist Dr. Reppersgaard, "The whole city slows down, people's concentration and work capacity reduce, and they are always tired." It's also when the least desirable elements of human nature come out, leading to a jump in drinking, crime, suicide, and accidents. Sleep-deprived, vitamin D–starved, inactive children develop more slowly intellectually and physically than they do in summer. Fewer babies are conceived during Mørketida. Many people find it hard to fall asleep each night. The sale of tranquilizers, sleeping pills, and amphetamines soars. Depression grows epidemic, and the moonless nights feel especially deep and desolate.

Sometime during the Bronze Age, people in the region began celebrating *Soldag*, "sun day," the official end of Mørketida, with prayers and animal sacrifice. It's still a major holiday today, when schools and businesses close early, and neighbors gather to drink "sun coffee" and "sun chocolate" while they await the dawn, which usually occurs at around 11:30 a.m. Randomly dipping into the Bible at dawn is said to foretell one's fate for the coming year. When the sun appears at last, cheers and tears ensue, it's heralded as "She," and people speak of "Her return." She doesn't linger long, doesn't climb the sky, just floats on the horizon for a brief reddish-yellow spell, and then darkness spills once more. But that's enough to renew belief in the coming of summer. Not that Arctic summer will offer much scope for basking. Between May 21 and July 23, the sun circles the sky without setting, and yet the hottest days don't beat 45 degrees. People stay outdoors as much as possible, swim in heated pools, ski, or hike, and some swear it makes them live more intensely, more mindfully, and more in touch with nature, since every sunlit day is precious.

Meanwhile, in Helsinki, Finland, during Mørketida, diners at Café Engel enter through faux Greek columns to find breakfast served, if they wish, with individual light boxes. *Eggs sunny-side up and a side order of dawn.* One light box shines 10,000 lux, the same as a spring sunrise. A sunny day at the beach showers us in 100,000 lux. An office's fluorescent shoals offer 500 lux. A typical room in one's house is lit to only 300 to 400 lux, but the brightest glow by far is shed by the TV set. More lux isn't just easier to read by, it feels more *luxurious*, it satisfies the ancient craving for light, one that soothed our edgy human minds for millennia. How strange that we time our days by a ball of fire in the sky and a cold dead white ghost of a moon.

FORGET BATS

⌒

A s the sun drives gold nails through the shadows, a dull red dawn, the color of deer and rust, soars up the sky. A hundred palm trees look like tufted pens in inkwells. A flock of slack-jawed pelicans glides overhead, perfectly aligned as synchronized swimmers. Brisk winds drive clouds overhead like time-lapse photography, and I feel the ancient thrill of impending sunlight.

Female boat-tailed grackles squeak like crib toys as they fly among the palms. Sitting in the poinciana trees, the males seem to be going down their checklist: *check, check, check, check.* One pair perches atop a curved frond of a palm tree, the female buzz-warbling while fluttering her unopened wings. Her mate ignores her, preens himself without joining in, despite her insistent invitation. Not in the mood? Passive-aggressive? We name, we interpret. But *feelings?* The ignored mate's frustration and distress are clear even to a human by its increasingly strident and snippy call.

Soon all the grackles are madly clamoring, some in a squeaky whinnying that sounds like the twisting of wet rope, as they fly fast and full of purpose carrying scraps of dry palm leaves to their roof-tile nests. A foot-long curlicue of leaf falls beside me on the chaise. Some nest-holder chose it as good building material. Matted fibers folded together while drying give it a tensile strength ideal for building hut or nest and a surprising softness. I place it on the railing in the sun where the bird who dropped it may chance upon it and feel whatever the grackle version is of pleased. Then I slowly comb my hair with open fingers, coaxing out any knots, and tuck the loosened hairs under the leaf for the grackle to use as insulation. I hear some people also put out lint from a clothes dryer to become nesting fluff. But most often we become part of avian nurseries without realizing how intricately we're woven into their world.

Flying fast from opposite directions, two grackles meet in midair, do a quick loop-the-loop around each other to synchronize wingbeats, and fly off in the same direction. Other birds work hard to stay aloft in the heavy morning air. A lone grackle twirls to the ground like an open penknife in a controlled spin. He makes it seem so soft, so casual, that terrifying spin that pilots pray they will correct well before the ground. I practiced a spin once (with an instructor) over the revolving fields of historic Virginia, and still remember the scrambled sky, sobering fright, and counterintuitive moves. Birds know instinctively how to fan their wide blunt tail feathers and glide on the collapsing wind. Or maybe only those survive who do know. Does a spin make a bird nauseous, as it does a human in a plane? Do birds excel at bird-in-flight recognition—by wing shape, flight rhythms—the whole "fizz" of a bird aloft? Probably so. Basic plane spotting. Part of their schooling as birds will be how to gauge the force of wind, learning by experience that some blows are unfordable, and others can be circled around or tacked into. The airmanship of birds involves lots of trial and error and what we might call reasoning or analysis. How that fills the bird brain with revisions and prompts I don't know, but their brains learn, adapt, and rewire as they grow. Such is the clout of having even the smallest brain.

A female grackle cleans her feathers, which must feel good; I doubt she understands the purpose of preening, that she can't fly safely if her plumage is grubby. She pays special attention to the tail's steering feathers and the wings' long stiff flight feathers. Each sweaty, parasite-laden day, some of the hooked-together barbs pull apart, and she must rezip them so that she doesn't lose lift. Everything also needs to be oiled, especially the flight feathers. Lots of aircraft maintance goes into being a grackle. Meanwhile, her monosyllabic mate sits nearby, caulking the seams of each minute: *caulk, caulk, caulk.* The pair calls and coos, then switches to short melodies and smoochy sounds. Having found their song, they begin a hoedown of flights, with jumps, cackles, clicks, pennywhistles, tsk-tsks, glottal stops, creaky wood, kookaburra crescendos, hyena laughs, trills, croaks, peeps, and quacks.

Among the hearty calls of adult birds, and the church bell ringing on the half hour, comes the frail high-pitched peep of nestlings tucked beneath the terracotta tiles overhead, pleading their bellies. Dozens of parent birds to-and-fro, greeted by the squeals of their hatchlings. Combining a buzzer, caw, and rattle, a female boat-tailed grackle pauses only a second on the ledge before setting out again for gobstoppers. She will need to find a bucketful by nightfall, and like a lioness, she will hunt single-mindedly to feed her young. Her mate rests on a nearby curb, making quick high-pitched whistles, as if he's summoning a taxi. In the bell tower, another female flies off with diapers (fecal sacs) cleared out from the nest, as a male lands with a long palm leaf in his mouth.

A sudden movement on the floor beside my chair catches my eye just as a baby grackle pogo-hops past. It looks up at me, then hides beneath the chair and begins chirping shrilly, using its slack yellow clown-mouth that, in time, will mature into a crisp strong beak. A parent calls back over and over. It's not hard to translate—something like *Help! I'm here, where are you?!* and *Over here!* When I stand up to scout its whereabouts, it has vanished, but I can still hear parent and chick calling, and trace the chick's call to a balcony about twenty feet away. Did it hop or fly there? Or both? It looks well-fledged and uninjured, so it must have glided clumsily down from the nest in at least a recovered fall. Running around, standing and shaking, calling plaintively, it seems frightened. Soon it will risk fluttering, winging. Chicks do. But a cityscape, however tropical, is not like a yard with lots of branches to hide in. Will a parent swoop down to feed it? No squirrels or raccoons clamber up here and attack it, no chipmunks or cats stalk it. But there are still marauding owls, jays, sparrows, ospreys, and hawks. I hear another chick's notes and track that one to the green feathered canopy of a palm. It sounds just as urgent, and it's staying close to home. The clamor of hungry baby birds and their frantic parents is never-ending.

Yes, I think, looking up at all the nests on the ledges above, *it will be raining baby birds for a while.* Even the curly-tailed geckos seem impressed, and let me tell you it takes a lot to impress a curly-tailed gecko. Some chicks will live, others crash and die. Best get used to it. In time the parents show up with quick confident turns and hard yellow beaks, landing together on the railing near the fallen chick. One at a time, they fly to it and fly back to the railing, showing it what to do. I have seen this monkey see, monkey do before, and always enjoy watching parents teaching their nestlings flight rules, including how to stall safely into a nest.

The next morning, as the fog of darkness lifts from the balcony, a pool of greater darkness catches my eye: a dead baby bird, fallen from a nest fifty feet up in the bell tower. Fully fledged, the chick has long legs, brownish-black feathers, and a bright yellow target of a mouth, slack and still. Ants have created wagon trails of scent leading to and from the dead chick. I hear the urgent hunger peeps of its siblings and I imagine its parents can do the simple math of one less mouth to feed. What do they feel when, searching for food, they see the dead chick lying lifeless, swarmed over by a thrill of ants? The living and the dead—these are hard distinctions for any raucous, vibrant being to master.

Another chick flops brokenly on the patio floor, heart visibly pounding as it keeps trying to right itself. Mother, looking thin and twitchy, hops along a railing close by and chirps to it in short contact calls of *I'm here, I'm here, come on, come on.* Now and then she drives off menacing sparrows. Even when, after several hours, the chick finally stops moving for good, the mother keeps calling a short wringing of wet fabric screech over and over.

It's hard to tell if the chick was pushed out of the nest by an older sibling ("An heir and a spare" being nature's motto), or was trying to fly before it was ready. To me, it looks like it has just enough wing feathers to glide, but what do I know of bird muscle or the feel of slick, smooth, air-hugging feathers, as opposed to the warm weak chaos of soft down? As a human several species away, brimming with mirror neurons that spur empathy, I only know: *Its avid eye has seen so little.*

And so life cycles on, with each generation born into a different universe, a sovereign intersection of time and space, history, mores, air quality, fads, dialect. Just as our skin cells slough off and are replaced every two weeks, our planet is regularly rebirded and repeopled, and the world those youngsters grow up into and influence is a unique combination of chance and circumstance that's largely unpredictable and inscrutable. Their parents can't fathom most of it, let alone prepare them for it. We all meet on our separate timelines like sliding panes of glass that crash at times. It's amazing we get on as well as we do. But empathy makes it possible, and love makes it worthwhile.

SOME TALES WE TELL

⟶

M ANY TOWNS INCLUDE A STREET named Aurora, after the Roman goddess of dawn, who renews herself daily and soars over the world, proclaiming the arrival of the sun, her brother Sol. Luna, the moon, is her sister. In Roman myth, where gods and goddesses enjoy mingling with humans, Aurora falls in love with Tithonus, the prince of Troy. But, wanting her love to last forever, she begs Zeus to allow Tithonus immortality. Zeus obliges, granting Aurora's plea in its narrowest form. Although love-smitten Aurora desired eternal life for her mate, she neglected to request eternal youth, and so Tithonus ages miserably, with cease-less pain. In some versions of the myth, she turns him into a cicada, and then instead of singing love songs he begs to be allowed to die.

In a newly found poem written 2,600 years ago, Greek poet Sappho gives voice to Tithonus's lament:

. . . my hair's turned [white] instead of dark;
my heart's grown heavy, my knees will not support me,
that once on a time were fleet for the dance as fawns.
This state I oft bemoan; but what's to do?
Not to grow old, being human, there's no way.
Tithonus once, the tale was, rose-armed Dawn,
love-smitten, carried off to the world's end,
handsome and young then, yet in time grey age
o'ertook him, husband of immortal wife.

                    (translation by Martin West)

Thanks to Homer, who gave the ancients some of their best imagery, "rosy-fingered" is how they imagined Dawn, a goddess mourning for someone still alive. This nearly complete poem of Sappho's was discovered in 2005 on paper wrapping a mummy, and if that sounds strange, bear in mind that's how all of Sappho's poems have come to us, as papier-mâché fragments from tombs. The great Library of Alexandria once held nine books of her poetry, including one poem of 1,320 lines, but today we have precious few, none of them complete. When the Library of Alexandria was sacked (historians differ on when and by whom), the scrolls containing Sappho's works were tossed onto a rubbish heap along with countless other "pagan" books, all to be recycled. Morticians preparing the dead for burial needed rags to clothe the bodies in, and so they ripped the scrolls lengthwise and used the strips on mummies. That's why we only have fragments of most of Sappho's poems, and odd fragments at that, with words missing vertically as well as horizontally.

I think Tennyson wrote the most beautiful poem about

Dawn and her lover, also a dramatic monologue spoken by Tithonus, which begins with these lines:

> The woods decay, the woods decay and fall,
> The vapors weep their burden to the ground,
> Man comes and tills the field and lies beneath,
> And after many a summer dies the swan.
> Me only cruel immortality
> Consumes: I wither slowly in thine arms,
> Here at the quiet limit of the world,
> A white-hair'd shadow roaming like a dream
> The ever-silent spaces of the East,
> Far-folded mists, and gleaming halls of morn.

When we say the word "dawn" or behold the gathering of light, we may not imagine the goddess and her tragic lover, may not believe her rosy fingers stir up trouble and the day. But for thousands of years, in sympathy and fear, people did believe that cautionary tale about our oldest human desire: endlessly renewing days, in which we waltz in time with Aurora.

The sky already seems light earlier as spring creeps north, blessed by Persephone, the ancient Greeks hoped, goddess of springtime and daughter of Zeus and Demeter. According to the myth, when she was out picking flowers one morning, Hades, lord of the underworld, stole her to be his wife. Her mother's tears killed the harvests and triggered a perpetual winter, and eventually Hades agreed to let Persephone leave the underworld for six months of each year, and so the seasons were born. Norse has Iduna as goddess of springtime and keeper of the heavenly orchard where the apples of immortality grow. What an odd way of imagining seasons, as entities with fickle tempers that arrive as gods and goddesses to sport with humble humans!

Science's story is that once, long ago, when Earth was a hatchling itself, a giant piece of space rubble hit our planet hard enough to leave it tilted and reeling as it orbits the sun, creating the seasons and our consort the Moon. I don't know if science's explanation is the real "truth," since nothing we think, see, do, analyze, measure, or wholeheartedly believe should ever be mistaken for *the* truth. Science is a tribute to our cleverness, but we are fallible and we filter out so much of the world. Our senses would be overloaded if they recorded the everythingness of everything. So metaphor is one of the brain's favorite ways of understanding the this and that of its surroundings, a kind of shorthand comparing the unknown to the known, which reminds us that we discover the world by engaging it and seeing what happens next. A lover in a "frosty" mood may yield a look that's withering and bleak. When something "dawns" on us, a stellar insight floats in the mind. Myth is a metaphor the brain tells in story form.

The companion myths of sun and moon, which dominated ancient religions, required a god for darkness and a god for light. Each needed the other to balance all the warring factions of the universe, all the opposites that seem to exist in nature: male and female, day and night, darkness and light, birth and death, winter and summer, desert and ocean, good and evil. In ancient China, everything on earth became either male or female at first light. Whichever side of an object the sun touched with its first life-giving rays automatically became *yang*, or male, and the dark side *yin*, or female. As a result, the east side of any mountain or skyscraper is considered female.

Believing in watchful gods, many of the ancients pictured the sun as a single eye peeking over the horizon at dawn. To the Greeks, the sun was the eye of *Zeus*; to the Teutons the eye of *Woden*; to the Sumatrans the eye of *Day*; to the Hindus the eye of *Varuna*; to the Persians the eye of *Ahura Mazda*. And, in the Rig-Vedas, the goddess of dawn bares her breasts to attract the eye of the sun god, so that he'll follow her torridly across the sky.

VENUS OBSERVED

⟜

A THIN CRESCENT MOON THAT GRAZED the constellation Pleiades at sunset now floats low on the eastern horizon. Below it hovers a single spark, a wanderer sometimes mistaken for a UFO. I look forward to finding Venus, the brightest celestial object, gracing the sky shortly before sunrise—a perennial beacon known as the Morning Star and Evening Star, or as our sister planet. Some sister. Hardly a love goddess, Venus stirs up a cauldron of sulfuric and hydrochloric acids, weird light shows, and a swelter hot enough to melt lead. But none of that is visible to the naked eye. Just before sunrise, it looks like a gem on the jeweler's velvet of the night, crisply dazzling and flanked by occasional shooting stars.

I like that Venus goes through phases like the Moon, and that its geographical features have been named after historical women. True, on Mars one can travel from Candor to Chaos (two place names) in a flash, but on Venus one finds a huge southern continent named Aphrodite, the Greek goddess of love, and a northern Australia-sized continent named Ishtar, the Babylonian goddess of love. That's only fitting. As far back as 1600 B.C., the Babylonians worshiped the goddess Venus as the embodiment of womanhood, a devotion literally carved in stone, on cuneiform tablets. The Hebrews called the planet *Noga* ("shining one") and also my favorite of her many names *Ayeleth-ha-Shakhar* ("deer of the dawn"). The best myth about Venus belongs to the Yolngu Aborigines of northern Australia, who tell how at dawn Venus pulls a rope of light behind her, one end fastened to the earth. All along that rope, people can talk with dead loved ones, and reassure them they're still remembered and cherished.

Long ago, during the aboriginal Dreamtime, Venus sang much of the land itself into existence and named the animals. Now, every morning, Walu (the Sun Woman) lights a torch to create the dawn. Then, dressing, she paints herself with red ochre, some of which spills onto the clouds. The Moon, Ngalindi, is a lazy fat man with two wives and two sons. Squabbling with his sons one day, he lost his temper and killed them, and when his wives found out they attacked him with axes, chopping off pieces of him. And so he wanes. Solar eclipses occur when the fat Moon Man hides the Sun Woman while making love with her.

I like that we use the planet's astronomical symbol, a circle with a cross beneath it, as the biological sign for female. In alchemy the same symbol stands for copper, what polished mirrors were made from in antiquity, which is why the goddess Venus is sometimes depicted holding a mirror. I like that Venus is intricately fractured and full of faults, eruptive, fiery, crusty at times, almost pristine in places, nowhere near as degraded as the Moon.

The Romans admired Venus's spangled brilliance in heralding dawn, a sight fetching enough to earn it the name Lucifer, from *lux*, *luc-*, "*light*," and *-fer*, "*bearing*." The only torment it brought to mind was Venus bedeviling mortals and immortals alike with red-hot love. How did Lucifer, the bright planet Venus, become Lucifer the devil? Search the Bible and the word Lucifer appears only once, in the Old Testament's Book of Isaiah, chapter 14, verse 12: "How art thou fallen from heaven, O Lucifer, Son of the morning! How art thou cut down to the ground which didst weaken the nations!"

Lucifer is never mentioned again in the Old or New Testament, but that instance was enough to launch Lucifer's career as diabolic fiend—the wicked, ungodly ruler of hell, famous for infernally blaspheming God, seducing (and sometimes impregnating) innocent girls, swiping souls, corrupting men through sinful pacts, requiring depraved rites of worship, putting up hell's own fight during exorcisms, and sowing the seeds for murder, mayhem, and chaos among humans whenever possible. Lucifer stars in countless paintings, songs, books, films, folklore, and of course fire-and-brimstone sermons.

But Lucifer is a Roman word, and the scribe who wrote the Book of Isaiah wrote in Hebraic. The Isaiah scribe's Lucifer is Helal, son of Shahar, a Babylonian king who persecuted the Israelites. His name translates as "shimmering one, son of the dawn," and Lucifer was simply a generic translation. Sun King has always been a popular nickname for monarchs, and though this one may well have been wicked, he was also mortal and, in time, deposed.

The trouble with the Christian idea of Lucifer the devil is that neither Jesus nor the early prophets believed in him. The idea of the devil originated later, and was based solely on the

King James Version of the Bible in English, when Lucifer was mistranslated on purpose, to help explain evil in the world and terrify anyone tempted by the wages of sin. That seems wickedly unfair to a dazzling planet, goddess of love and aboriginal liaison between the living and the dead. One can picture Venus as a woman with a past, or as a hellishly fascinating world, but either way the planet drags a rope of light after it, in what for some people is dream time, others is Dreamtime, and for the likes of me is that dreamy time just before dawn.

IN THE SPIRIT OF MONET

~

O N A CHILLY MORNING IN 1892, Claude Monet settled his
easel beside an open window in a rented second-story
room in Rouen, and began painting the Gothic cathedral
across the street, a soaring mountain of architecture he fondly
referred to as his "cliff." He had just finished his *Haystacks*
and *Poplars* series, in which he'd lavishly recorded the fugitive
spell of dawn, noon, and dusk alighting on a field. By layering two-dimensional canvases with three-dimensional paints,
he hoped to reveal a fourth dimension: time. "The older I
become," he wrote to his friend Georges Clemenceau, "the
more I realize I have to work very hard to reproduce what I
seek: the *instantaneous*."

In the end, Monet painted thirty-one dreamlike visions of
Rouen Cathedral, in thickly applied pigments that trail the
elusive migration of sunlight as it seeps into the stony recesses
and floods the shadows, creating an effect like the thick spill-

age left by dripping candles. By adding the element of change over time, he imbued the series with a cinematic rhythm.

Rising at 5:00 a.m. each day, Monet was a man of the dawn, and there were infinite dawns to capture, solidify in paint, and hang in the gallery of memory like souvenirs from neighboring countries, each with its own climate. Sixty vagabond dawns live in each minute, thirty ripening dawns in half an hour. Can one capture time-fragments? Surviving the death of an adored son and a beloved wife, Monet must have known how impossible that was. Yet he painted as many as fourteen canvases simultaneously in his rented rooms, recording the dynamic semblances of light. It was perceptions he chronicled, the atmospherics of living, rather than the reality of objects. As photons rain on stony edges, a cathedral changes in the mind, seamlessly, right up to that standstill when one's universe dies and one's conversation with the sun ends. But until then there are only spells of being so fleeting it's nearly impossible to retrieve them, even with the impasto of memory. They simply vanish into the psyche's library of lost things.

Once the brain notices something, we're primed to recognize it faster the next time, and even faster after that, until we needn't look at it carefully again. Visitors to a locale often see things the locals miss, especially if they're on holiday, with the sole purpose of just looking, noticing details, remembering. Babies, beginners, newcomers, artists, and mystics have this in common: unjaded eyes. Maybe that's why artists so often feel like outsiders—in every sense, they are perpetual tourists. Our perceptions fly under the radar most of the time, unless an artist like Monet wakes us and says, *Pay attention! Let me show you the transient beauty of absolutely any moment. Here is a wave. This is the rain.*

Moments tremble like the meniscus atop too-full glasses of water, bright domes of reflection swollen with life and ready to spill away. Likewise, we tremble, we brim, we fall. By freezing those continuums solid in color, Monet could revisit the *instantaneous*, idylls so sense-stealing that thought creaks to a halt, the senses stammer something like *light, light, light*, and, for a while anyway, all the hounds of time heel.

Then the canvas of our awareness fills with a vastness so ancient, astonishing, and visceral that we can neither understand nor turn away from it because it speaks a dialect of bone, whispers through our cells with revelry and relief about the joy of finding oneself alive, *again*, on one more morning, as night sails off, replaced by a floating world of color and birdsong.

Suffering, loss, and decay also arrive, pulling heavy barges. But at the moment (literally), those exist in another loch of perception, replaced by dawn on Sunrise Avenue, in Palm Beach, Florida, with many appearances by collared doves, flocks of feral parakeets, leopard geckos, humans, and other Palm Coast denizens. Or dawn at the end of a wooded cul-de-sac among the Finger Lakes of upstate New York, a quiet hummock of life honeyed over by ninety thousand working bees, visited daily by a local herd of deer, complete with a broad-bellied, multistoried old magnolia, and a street full of leggy, multistoried humans. Or dawn in India, Norway, or Bali. If we're lucky, we compass many of life's dominions. For a short spell, little more than a visitation really, I'm busy patrolling the dawn.

Surely Monet has been up for hours painting this watercolor sky in full cloud regatta. He limned many weatherscapes, but like the other Impressionists, preferred the sparkling blue skies of early morning when the air is tranquil. One can tell the time of day by the small puffy clouds that stalk their paintings, sometimes with wispy clouds higher above. Even in Paris, where pollution chalked the view, they tended to paint nearly empty skies with small well-behaved cumuli that haven't had time yet to swell in the hot humid afternoon haze.

Even though the Impressionists doted on clouds, they also liked to use broad heavy brushstrokes, so one rarely finds the delicate skeins of cirrus clouds in their skies. Not true for Monet, who would follow a cloudscape as it changed, during one day, over several canvases. I think he would have felt kinship with his American contemporary John Muir, who wrote of clouds that "come and go like living creatures looking for work," and reported tying himself high up the trunk of a tree during a thunderstorm, the better to understand both thunderstorm and tree, or maybe just for the thrill. "When the sun is shining—white, yellow, green, blue, vermillion, and other shades of red indefinitely blending," he said of Yellowstone Park, "all the earth hereabouts seems to be paint." He continued describing the glorious landscape in such watercolor terms as "the Nation's Art Gallery," and soon an illusion of painters fixed studios there for inspiration.

But Monet also loved the dreamlike miasma of polluted places—the Seine, which carried the effluvia and industrial waste of Paris, and London's sooty fog and pink factory plumes, which immersed its landmarks in many swirling colors, which he painted in nearly a hundred views between 1899 and 1901. "The Thames was all gold," he wrote to his wife, Alice, waiting in France. "God it was beautiful, so fine that I began to work in a frenzy, following the sun and its reflections on the water. . . . Thanks to the smoke a fog descended." He painted the Parliament houses so often, in carefully detailed études of color and sun, that one can almost use the series astronomically, as an *analemma*, the figure-eight path the sun makes in the sky.

Monet didn't mean to give Impressionism its name when, for a group exhibition in 1874, he titled one of his hypnotically atmospheric paintings *Impression, Sunrise*, which sounds a bit static in its English translation. The French title *Impression, soleil levant* conveys more of the magic of sunrise, when an orange-red ball levitates before one's eyes. Perched beside his window in Le Havre, he painted the harbor at dawn, on a misty morning, when sun and sky shone equally luminous and a simple squiggle of black was enough to create a fisherman in the foreground.

When a critic denounced the painting as mere "impression-ism," Monet and his friends adopted the label with perverse delight. For Monet, Renoir, and Pissarro, who would go on to show paintings together eight times, meticulously crafted impressions were exactly what they sought. The experience of being alive is only one impression after another, a feast for the senses in ever-changing light, one *now* seamlessly flowing into the next moment of being. How do you explore the texture of being alive? In *Impression, Sunrise*, Monet paints the lavish spell of the senses detained by a pink and blue sunrise, colors that create purple where they meet, in a softly puzzling war of blue and red that's not so much hue as emotion, as the eye struggles to make sense of it but pleasures in the ambiguity, and where a slightly out-of-focus fisherman floats in his own reality (no doubt occasionally eyeing the painter on the dock), and the rising sun is a wavery fireball at the end of a long path of copper cobblestones.

"Impressionism" was the perfect emblem for Monet's tribe

of sensates, which included the English painter J. M. W. Turner, who strapped himelf to the mast of a boat during a thunderstorm so that he could fully experience it. It included Marcel Proust, a born voluptuary, who intuited worlds of memory recorded by the body, through the senses, indelible as tattoos. It included Virginia Woolf, who explored life's elastic minutes. Monet simply proclaimed, and adored, what we all experience from moment to moment: the wash of sensations that greet us on waking, and which we try, at our cost, to dismiss as wasteful, self-indulgent, unproductive, or by some other term designed to separate us from our true self. The freedom of unbridling that self and losing it in nature is immeasureable. Alive moments can be anytime, anywhere. If I closely watch any natural wonder, really watch it, nonjudgmentally, in the present moment, noting its nuances, how it looks in changing light, or on different days, yet remains recognizably the same, then the world becomes dearer and less trying, and priorities rearrange themselves with an almost audible clicking.

In 1893, Monet began his most sensuous and evocative series of paintings, *Mornings on the Seine*. Rising early, he would climb into the boat he'd transformed into a floating studio, and set out on the river, painting the sensations of dawn in thick, voluptuous swirls of color riddled with light. Flanked by several easels and canvases, he floated, hidden from the eyes of neighbors but intimately a part of the water world, inserted into the landscape. These paintings, like many of Monet's, have no foreground, since he's afloat, standing next to his subject; and so, as viewers, we melt into the canvas and feel the live present river flowing through Monet's eyes. Ricocheting colors play straight onto the harp of the senses. Working at home later, he textured the canvases with the heavy stains of memory, using thick daubs of pure color. The paintings exist like Debussy's or Delius's music, as the tapestry of a changing mood. Monet hoped to capture the intimate drama of seeing something for the first time, create reverie and fluidity in pigments. How do you reacquaint the eyes? In sunrise paintings that play with color and somnambulisms of light.

In *Impression, Sunrise*, a brilliant orange sun ball throbs with motion, the whole painting pulses and shimmers. Painters con the brain with such sleights of mind, tricks of color and light that confuse our "What" and "Where" systems. My brain's "What" system enables me to see colors and decipher faces and objects. I detect the distinctly orange sun against the misty green-gray sky. A parallel "Where" system is color-blind but perceives small changes in brightness, revealing an object's location, speed, and depth. Because the sun and sky in Monet's painting are equally bright, the sun is invisible to the "Where" system. Struggling to make sense of things, my brain tries juggling colorful details with ill-defined position and movement, and vision jams, the eyes don't know what to see, and the painting seems to vibrate or pulse. In that way, he creates the optical illusion of twinkling stars, waving grass, throbbing suns, and shimmery seascapes. Monet once said of his water landscapes: 'They reveal the instability of a universe transforming itself every moment before our eyes."

"Everything sacred must surround itself in mystery," his poet friend Stéphane Mallarmé advised a generation; one should seek to create "not the thing but the effect it produces." In Monet's paintings, voluptuous veils of color invite the viewer into a silent, private world ripe for meditation, open to reflection. What could satisfy the mind after that?

FESTIVALS OF THE DAWN

—

WE STILL WORSHIP THE SUN, as a stroll down any street beside tanned, bare-fleshed humans shows. Religious rites, prayers, and festivals often take place at dawn and many involve water to cleanse the body as light cleanses the mind. In the Catholic tradition, at dawn one prays *Lauds* ("praises"), one of the two major canonical hours, a practice that can be traced back to the Apostles. Through the years, it's also been called the *Office of Cock-crow* and the *Office of the Resurrection of Christ*, since Christ supposedly rose from his tomb at dawn as "Conqueror of Death and of the Night." The prayer is to Christ as the "True Light," a canticle to be chanted as the sun begins to rise.

Now the sun looms in slow reverberations of yellow, like a monk chanting a mantra of light. In Sanskrit, the prefix *man-* means "think" or "have in mind." The suffix *-tra* means "tool" or "instrument." So a mantra is literally "a mind tool." One designed to pull dawn from darkness in a sudden flood of *enlightenment,* which literally means "light flooding into." A state when the world seems brighter than before, fully lit for the first time after a long starless night, a word that captures some of the fierce glare of sunrise, when truth *dawns.* Then light pierces the cobwebs we spin to protect ourselves. On the path to this enlightenment, Buddhist morning worship usually includes chanting, incense, and the ringing of a metal bowl. But in some monasteries, monks rise before dawn and meditate until they can make out the lines on their palms, then put on their robes in the twilight and walk in silence to nearby villages, where they beg for alms, their only food for the day.

The Jewish liturgy includes a list of blessings to be said upon arising, which begins by thanking God for giving roosters enough intelligence to tell day from night. Then the keystone prayer of the *Shema* is to be chanted 'as soon as there is light enough to recognize an acquaintance standing six feet away," which they say occurs at exactly thirty-five minutes before sunrise.

At dawn, ancient Egyptians celebrated the Feast of Nut, mother of the sun god Ra, who changed himself into the god of the sunrise, Khepera, whose name means "to become." He's usually shown with a beetle on his head, or a beetle *as* his head. Khepera is the dawn embodied, a god who rolls the sun across the sky much as a dung beetle rolls a ball of dung, pushing the ball into a hole and laying her eggs there so that her emerging larvae can feast. Long ago, Egyptians noticed the hatchlings geysering up from the earth, heaving themselves into existence, and decreed Khephera a god with a gift of self-invention and rebirth.

A muezzin calls Muslims to prayer at dawn, and before each of the five daily prayers scripture says one should bathe head, hands, forearms, and feet in a fountain that mosques usually provide for such ablutions. In Japan, a dawn visit to a Shinto shrine also begins with a purification ritual—scooping up water from a basin to clean the hands and mouth. The first Shinto ritual of the year takes place at dawn on New Year's Day, when the emperor goes into the palace sanctuary, performs the *Prayer to the Four Quarters*, then prays for the welfare of his nation. And the Hindu Kumbh Mela festival— the largest religious gathering on earth—always begins with purification by bathing in the Ganges at dawn.

On Kumbh Mela morning in Allahabad, India, the sun rises like a gold medallion over the brow of the river, where, as the fog rolls away and the first funeral pyres are being lit, holy men of various Hindu sects begin arriving in cars, chariots, and litters, atop camels and horses, to descend the *ghats*—long shallow staircases leading down to the river. First light brings clarity and the world becomes real as golden rays touch everything, including the bathers whose cold flesh they warm.

We may bathe in the sun, but only water has the power to dispel wickedness, forgive villainy, and cleanse a thoroughly depraved soul. In France, grotto water from Lourdes supposedly heals the sick. In India, bathing in the Ganges is said to rinse away sins, clarify doubts, and cure illness. So robust is its power that even a drop added to tap water endows it with holiness, and Hindus immerse themselves, the ashes of loved ones, and sacred objects in the heavily polluted Ganges. Water from the river purifies sites, and bathing in the waters at the holy town of Haridwar is said to pardon any abomination, even murdering a holy man.

It makes sense that we're drawn down to rivers at sunrise for rebirth—the placental memory of water ghosts through our cells, as does the release of waters breaking. Only the thinnest layers of skin separate our gush from its, our minute currents from its thick ropy ones, and our travels—both physical and immaterial—from its peregrinations. Like dawn, a river rises out of some unknown darkness, crosses the threshold of the visible world, becomes brilliantly lit and present for a spell full of light and life, then travels to an unknown place. In Wales a sacred haunt of druids bears the longest name in the world—LLANFAIRPWLGWYNGYLLGOGERYCHWYRNDROB-WLLLLANTYSILIOGOGOGOCH, which means: "Saint Mary's Church in the hollow of the white hazel near a rapid whirlpool and the Church of Saint Tysilio of the red cave." Nothing is fathomable without water, since *fathoming* is the ancient way to measure water, in units of a *fathom*, the distance between a pair of outstretched arms. A river moves like one animal; its coolness isn't separate from its smoothness or flow.

The dark undulating Ganges easily takes shape in imagination as a voluptuous female deity who, like most deities, is bribable and licensed to grant wishes. Some Bengalis invite Mother Ganga to bless a marriage: the day before the wedding, the bride and her female relatives offer gifts to the river in a special cutting ritual. One of the women wades into the water, carrying a knife, and ceremoniously slashes the waves open, as if she means to bleed the river before inserting flowers and other gifts. On the morning of the wedding, they return to collect river water for use during the ceremony, mainly to bless the couple, but maybe also to acquit them of any small infamies that might taint the holy union.

Ashes to ashes, dust to dust, Westerners say. For Hindus that would be *ashes to water*, and at dawn one sees the first funeral pyres lit along the river. Grief-stricken families may travel far to cremate a loved one beside the Ganges, boulevard to heaven, a pilgrimage that also grants the otherwise helpless mourners some peace. As ashes spill into the water, the departed find freedom from the tyranny of birth and death by sidestepping reincarnation and proceeding straight to enlightenment.

People blend the ashes of their dead in the Ganges, sanctify marriages, and bless newborns, so it touches every stage of life. When pilgrims come down to the river at dawn, cleanse the road weariness and sweat from their bodies, and chant prayers in the rising light, they stir the waters of life and death by wading into them and willingly dissolve in mystery, not finally, not all at once, but physically and symbolically, shedding the old self cell by cell.

The Ganges has many lives, dawning in an ice cave under a glacier on India's border with China and winding through China, India, Nepal, and Bangladesh, while irrigating rice fields and farmlands, carrying tons of silt, flowing all the way to the huge delta and the Sunderbans. In that swamp forest, tigers attack people in boats so often that fishermen have started wearing masks on the backs of their heads to deter them by appearing big-eyed and vigilant.

At intervals, Mother Ganga calls all her children home, down to the banks of the river to purify themselves, and 70 million obey, making a heavenly racket. There's nothing quite like the noise of surrendered sin. Biding by Vedic astrology, Kumbh Mela takes place four times during a twelve-year cycle, when the planet Jupiter enters the house of Aquarius while the Sun enters Aries at dawn. During that auspicious time, the festival rotates among four cities on the banks of the Ganges: Allahabad, Haridwar, Ujjain, and Nashik. In 1895 Mark Twain attended the Kumbh Mela, and I can picture him entering the hubbub wearing the white suit and hat he always wore everywhere, which would quickly have changed color from dust, sweat, curry, henna, river water, and ashes. He would have rubbed elbows with a procession of millions, including gurus, monks, ash-smeared ascetics, Africans with lips stretched around plates, the Jangam order of wandering monks who wear peacock-feathered turbans, politicians, luminaries, the deeply devout, and the simply curious.

These days, some holy men arrive on gilded litters under gold-painted umbrellas. Elephants have now been banned (too dangerous), so some saints ride in chariots pulled by tractors. Following the holy men, tens of thousands of believers swarm as one organism, singing and chanting, praying and cheering as a red ball dances on the horizon.

The first monks plunge into the cold, grime-dark river, dipping themselves repeatedly as the crowd, held back by mounted police and a barricade of tree trunks, tosses them garlands of marigolds. After the monks have bathed and worldly shapes become visible, others may wade into the river to rinse away their sins and pray for peace and rebirth, for both themselves and the planet. In the land of an acknowledged caste system (in contrast to the implicit ones in other countries), different facilities exist for the most humble up to the VIP, with tents booked well ahead of time. Closed-circuit television screens in a central control booth monitor the chafe of crowds, the traffic control towers, and the parking lots where vehicles are grouped according to size and speed. River police in motorboats guide pilgrims arriving by water in darkness.

The next Kumbh Mela will take place in April 2010, in

the northern Indian city of Haridwar, in the foothills of the Himalayas, starting at sunrise, when the largest crowds will assemble to follow holy men down to the river and bathe. How will a city that normally supports 2 million people host 70 million? It will happen by dawn's light, with prayer, misdeed, and bloodshed, and in full knowledge for once that in time everything, everyone, and every deed will be washed away.

TROUBADOURS

〜

Not knowing when the dawn will come
I open every door;
Or has it feathers like a bird,
Or billows like a shore?

—EMILY DICKINSON, LXXXIX

IN THE TWILIGHT WORLD, A full moon looks close and touchable as a piñata. The first few birds begin testing out their songs, while humans hum in the shower and warm up their voices, too, with snags of melody or tuneless whistles. As the low lights of dawn filter in like news from a far country, a gray sky becomes visible. One wren sings a little more stridently than usual, chalking out his domain with noise. What would the human equivalent be—a man standing outside his house yelling, *Keep away! This is my turf!?* We have so many ways to stake a claim or show custody. A bird has a voice, an invisible fence it must hammer at throughout the day. Lucky for us that voice sounds agreeable.

Five minutes later, half a dozen birds join the chorus: some pipe delicate tentative song fragments, others tweedle and twitter emphatically. A single crow whacks out a *caw, caw, caw,*

caw. A monk parakeet sounds like it's prying the lid off a can of motor oil. A phoebe begins darning a hole in the sky. It's funny hearing birds trying out parts of their song as they wake, or perhaps *to* wake. I love this warm-up, wake-up, speaking in tongues at sunrise, when creatures discover they've survived another night on this sun-and-storm, human-battered planet and, not knowing what to say about it, or needing to say anything, just babble for a while. Birds babble. Baby birds before they learn their songs, and sleepy adult birds before they've cranked up the old tunes. They all babble as we do while stumbling around in mental fog.

Sooty gray pigeons land on the roof and quack once like ducks. Are they talking to convey something or simply enjoying *talanoa*, the Fijian word for idle talk as a social adhesive? It may be their sort of "Hi, Joe." The nesting boat-tailed grackles fill the air with back talk, dares, chants, building codes, rah-rah cheers, kibitzing, work songs, and urgent bubbling exclamations. When one of their mob flies off for construction materials, they hush briefly.

At 5:44 a.m. more droplets of birdsong materialize, quickly joined by slips of trill, plunking river pebbles, and burbled syllables. These begin as trickle, small rivulets of song, probably not so much yawns as vocal stretches. By 5:55 a.m., birds have strung slivers of verbiage into longer phrases, but I hear no complete melodies. One wren cranks out staccato notes, a chirp repeated until the tune flows more smoothly and faster. No warble yet, no war dance, boast, existential *I am*, or serenade. Just thumbtacks of sound until the throat loosens, the brain remembers, and it sings.

Then, as the sky fades from night purple to brilliant forget-me-not blue, a pandemonium of warbles erupts. It sounds like all the members of an opera chorus rehearsing different roles at the same time, oblivious to one another. But, of course, I'm missing its subtleties, since birds tailor their songs to their landscape. Just as shepherds on the Canary Islands whistle to one another across the long valleys, birds use far-carrying songs to contact family, friends, and rivals—a band of invisible others too remote to see or too hidden deep in vegetation. Through song, they stay audible as they flap from aerial to invisible.

Birds sing into their landscape, piercing it with sound. In a dense forest canopy, where notes are muffled by foliage, high quick sharp songs slice through the leaves. But in open fields the red-winged blackbird perches on branch or fence and buzzes kazoo-like dares for miles, and the finch trills as it soars above a meadow, letting its message rain down. It takes strength and real work to sing loudly, which also tells predators of its whereabouts, and so a bold song usually means a clever fighter or escape artist. Like our troubadours, avian males win their paramours with song, and birdsong doesn't lie. Despite our limited lung power and vocal range, we crafty humans, on the other hand, lie elaborately and well, exaggerating our talents with microphones, amplifiers, instruments, and computers. We've created tools as detachable organs. Our singers also duel for importance, and the winners rarely want for mates. Our sound box sits high atop the trachea, but the bird's equivalent, the syrinx, lies farther down where the windpipe branches into each lung. There, thin membranes tremble as air blows over them and birds can pipe two different sounds at the same time, mix the tones, vary the beat. Muscles shape the sounds, with the strongest birds fashioning the most intricate or innovative songs, some becoming one-bird marching bands.

After night's speckled dark, this splash of birdsong excites.

Every bird on earth seems to have arrived at the same party at the same time, cackling and hooting, singing and jawing, laughing and whistling. They do not mean to sound so beautiful to human ears. Just as a mother bat returning from a night banquet can detect the scent of her pup in a cave of a million rock-hugging young, and a human can recognize the voice of a friend on a crowded beach, each bird pinpoints the call of its partner, pals, or young. Do they notice all the noise and competing songs? I imagine so, just as we do. A knack for paying attention, one of evolution's best gifts, works so well that nature has sized it for all living things according to their needs. Even slugs will stand up and pay attention if you really startle them.

6:26 a.m. A full throaty wren sings, followed by a chipping reply. *Hey gal. You awake? You awake?* Answered by *I am, I am, I am!*

Excited to see the sun once more, a song great within them, birds can't help but sing. Maybe it's the raw animal joy of surviving the night, and the pleasure of having a body to stretch and bend and sing awake. At dawn, there's less wind and noise to baffle sound, and less light so they're not tempted to hunt. By singing at low ebb after a nightlong fast, a male bird boasts about his strength. Any animal that wakes with a song (including humans) shows good health and energy abounding to protect home and mate.

With rivals close at hand, males claim their turf with song lines, and rivals are always close, taking the stage and warbling into their territory from various angles. Now and then they pause to listen for naysayers, and can easily tell a cranky but familiar neighbor from a stranger posing a serious threat. Only single males wage this tunefest, and since females like variety—long songs with complex stylings—they mate first with the best crooners. As a result, bachelor birds sometimes duel in song.

To that end, the brown thrasher is endowed with the biggest repertoire (over two thousand songs), but the pert little sedge warbler can pipe long full-throated arias, mixing fifty-some elements to design brand-new songs, one after the other, for its entire career. Mind you, female birds sometimes sing, too. The lady red-winged blackbird, for instance, serenades her mate with one song and chases off rival females with another song. Whooper swans, Canada geese, and African shrikes perform intricate duets, and in a pinch, or when grieving, will sing the partner's half of their poignant song.

But for sheer variety, none exceeds the mockingbird, the cheerleader of the morning, who wakes all the other birds by reminding them of their songs. It's a sort of roll call—and from such an unassuming bird the color of chestnuts, which doesn't open its mouth very wide or overinflate its chest or read from a score. It may also imitate a car alarm, a hodgepodge of air-conditioners, the occasional *chomp* of a car door closing and latching, or an airplane climbing out. Any of these sounds can enter the dawn chorus as an avian version of found poetry. But it mainly sticks to whistle toots and peeps, mixed with squawk, twitter, trill—with pencil sharpening, nutmeg being scraped, and bicycle bells thrown in for good measure. Sometimes it will borrow police siren, dump truck, motorcycle. It becomes a jukebox, a solo opera. I've never heard one go *meow* or *woof*, but for all I know that may be happening somewhere right now. Knitting phrases together, it chooses ones that segue smoothly into each other, whatever that means for a mocking-bird, given its anatomy and aesthetics. Do mockingbirds have aesthetics? They must, or they would choose any old sound and create an unspeakable mess. Their jazzy medleys must feel good in the throat and the brain. What does music feel like vibrating a bird's hollow bones? The nearest I can imagine is the time I slipped from a boat into the ocean near Hawaii, heard the siren song of humpback whales and felt their songs vibrating my rib cage. But that dazzled by being strange. A bird would find its song as commonplace a sensation as we do the breathiness of talk. I don't know how it masters the blackbird's buzz-twang, the wren's sweet adagios, the sparrow's liquid whistle, the monk parakeet's insane harmonica. You'd expect a mockingbird to have a suitcaseful of sound-effects gadgets like some avian DJ.

This morning, one lone mockingbird sits atop a telephone wire, testing out its full repertoire, a dictionary compendium under "birdsong" which it hurls into the faint light. Some of the hoots, jibbers, and melodic pirouettes are new to me. *Mimus polyglottos*, the polyglot mimic. It trills and warbles, yodels and sighs, buzzes and caws in a single ribbon of magically changing song. It has a long stiff slender tail, a white lightning bolt on each wing, an oily-looking eye it seems to have ringed with eyeliner, and when it swells its throat for even the simplest peep notes, two tiny black feathers erect from its white throat feathers. Like a ventriloquist minus the dummy, it runs through its routine. It's as if one actor spoke all of a play's roles at speed in several languages. Small wonder the Cherokees named mockingbirds *cencontlatolly* ("four hundred tongues"), or *hushi balbaka* ("bird that speaks a foreign language"), and fed mockingbird hearts to their toddlers to help them learn language.

At one point, a female cardinal lands nearby, catches sight

of the voice-masked suitor, and flies off. *Tricked again. Another wannabe cardinal, a mockingbird in cardinal's-song clothing.*

The mockingbird has the stage all by itself for a solid minute while it tests a wardrobe of even more phrases borrowed from other birds and non-birds, too, stitching them together into one broad avian sampler.

By 6:32 an aurora of pink and blue stripes seems to be emanating from the east, where long cloud fingers comb the sky. Another mockingbird blazes into sight, zooming through barnstorming loops. Gliding down to a fence next to a dense hedge, it settles beside its mate. They've chosen a hidden nest, but one right in the thick of things. When a woman appears walking a white Maltese dog, the male mockingbird hops to the ground and lowers its wing tips, spreads its tail sharply until white feathers show, and waggles the tail up and down, then side to side like a cautionary finger. The dog yips with coal eyes flashing, and the bird back-flaps furiously over the dog, which jumps at it until the bird flies back to its perch. With chicks in the nest, mockingbirds will dive-bomb most any real or imaginary threat, regardless of size: birds, dogs, snakes, people, bicycles. That's why, in 1927, Texas named the mockingbird its state bird with the declaration "It's a fighter for the protection of his home, falling, if need be, in its defense, like any true Texan." I like hearing the young's faint breathy peeps as I pass, don't mind scolding by the male, who has attacked me but never drawn blood. I tried removing my sun hat in case he saw it as a sort of raised crest, but it made no difference.

The brittle moon looks frozen in place. A bus growls by, followed by the surf of passing cars, the distant squealing of brakes, the whirling whistle of an ambulance. The mockingbird goes right on yapping, joined by countless other birds crooning their equivalent of *Come hither*, or *I am*, as the sky blues up and a pale fire searches the eastern face of almost everything. Soon the dawn chorus builds into a huge crescendo, and then a gold doubloon levitates in the sky.

MISSIVE

～

A N ANCIENT DEFINITION OF DAWN is the moment when
one can recognize the face of a friend. A morning phone
call delivers the news of the death of John O'Donohue, lark-
tongued Celtic poet, philosopher, theologian, ex-priest, and
what the Irish call an *anam cara*, a soul friend. At first my
brain denies the hearsay and refuses to add it to its library of
facts. In shock and disbelief, my brain trips all over itself, then
I feel the sudden monstrous subtraction that comes with the
death of parent, child, grandparent, sweetheart, special friend.
Two and two no longer equal four, the world comes unhinged
and a draft blows through it. I may grow old enough to know
many loved ones who didn't wake to see the dawn, but I feel
fortunate to have had a friend as divinely articulate as John,
someone so in tune with life.

He loved the *thisness* of things, as well as their poetry,
and especially loved thresholds and awakenings and dawn.
"If you had never been to the world and never known what

dawn was," John once said, "you couldn't possibly imagine how the darkness breaks, how the mystery and color of a new day arrive."

"Subversive" was a perfectly odd and daring word that he favored, one that evoked an insurgency of belief, an insurrection against habitual ways of knowing, a charity of awareness, blessed by the heart's iambic, despite the ego-mad *I am*'s of everyday life. Presence mattered, perhaps more than anything, because he understood the tragedy of being absent from one's own life.

I loved John's belief in the feral soul of poetry. He found poetry a kind of attentiveness, a form of endless rebirth, a mystical path to the divine. He understood, as truly as glass understands light, the ability of poetry to heal a mutilated world. And so he practiced dharma poetics, poetry as a vehicle of awakening.

The first Irish poem, declaimed by Amairgen in 1700 B.C., as he stepped onto shore and claimed the land for his people, presents his spiritual and supernatural heart:

> *I am the wind which breathes upon the sea,*
> *I am the wave of the ocean,*
> *I am the murmur of the billows,*
> *I am the ox of the seven combats,*
> *I am the vulture upon the rocks,*
> *I am the beam of the sun,*
> *I am the fairest of plants,*
> *I am the wild boar in valour,*
> *I am the salmon in the water,*
> *I am a lake in the plain,*
> *I am a world of knowledge,*

I am the point of the lance of battle,
I am the God who created the fire in the head.

"This ancient poem," John writes in *Anam Cara*, "preempts and reverses the lonely helplessness of Descartes's 'cogito ergo sum,' I think therefore I am. For Amairgen, I am because everything else is. I am in everything and everything is in me. It is a oneness first known between mother and child."

We once spent a day co-teaching a workshop called "Awakening the Senses, Romancing the Words." We focused on how the lamp of art allows one to shine light into dark corners, glimpse the intangible, spell beauty, and pan through the flow of experience for nuggets of illumination. This was a writing workshop about paying close attention to life, using poetry, story, myth, and meditation to honor the call of beauty and develop our capacity to find it in the most unexpected places.

I called him OJohn, and we were slated to meet at a symposium a few months from now, and again at a mindfulness retreat in late fall. I already lament those missed reunions and confluence of hearts and minds. But mainly I feel lucky to have known one of life's sublime celebrants for a few of his dawns. In the spirit of his poetic *Blessings*: May your mornings greet you with such a friend.

John's poetry and prose is so deliciously smeared with the senses that I can picture him now, fiercely alive with the electric fizz of being, not dead, just out of reach for a while, writing in his seaside house in Connemara, Ireland. My mind furnishes his house and places him in it, as it always has—how can he not be there now?

OJohn, the first light this morning that doesn't shine

for you hangs on the air like old yellowed linen. Shouldn't there be scarlet banners celebrating your passionate verve? Or at least a plume of color staining the sky the way you left your imprint on everyone, reaching deep into them, finding their state of highest grace, and helping them rise to it? You knew the best one could become, the plateaus of being, and the thresholds that arise, frighten, but must be crossed to become the self one dreams. I didn't know you often, but deeply, as a pilgrim side of me.

On the last evening of your life, you slept with your fiancée, Kristine, felt saturated with joy, having spent the happiest day. You were that rare man who met the girl of his dreams and stayed happy for the rest of his life—but only a few hours remained of it. You were fifty-three, planning a marriage, picturing the faces of the children you hoped for, full of a thousand blessings. For hundreds of thousands of years, most of our time on this planet, people could expect a lifespan of only eighteen years, still, fifty-three seems shockingly few.

Everyone who ever spent time with you came away changed. It's not that you were nobler than other noble souls, or more devout, or kinder, or more reverent. You drank too much, were prankish, could be hilariously irreverent. But you lived your words about being present in the world, you were able to be utterly alive in an era of distractions.

Had you awakened, you would have found the sky right where you left it, the way we all do, your sweetheart beside you, nestled in the aura of romantic love with all its hallelujahs. Your future included a new collection of poetry and prose called *Blessing the Space Between Us*, and the silent blessings of all your students and readers, the newlyweds whose vows you blessed, the mourners whose loved ones you buried, the parents whose newborns you helped christen. and the flock of spiritual seekers whose hunger you fed.

We all died last night, as we do every night. Waking is always a resurrection after what might have been death. What would dawn have been like, had you awakened? It would have sung through your bones. All I can do this morning is let it sing through mine.

RED DAWNS AND
FIELDS OF GREEN

～

A TUMULTUOUS BRUISE FLOATS OVER THE horizon, creating a color that hovers between red and blue, not really either, or neither, but an ambiguity of sensation that makes the eyes tremble with uncertainty. We call this event *purple*. When it's bright enough to see things clearly, nature becomes green again. Earth life equals green everywhere I look, from the ghostly greens of new shoots and beans to the cavernous green of aged leaves. We just happen to live on a world where plants broadcast green. Using sunlight, they mint organic compounds through the pigment chlorophyll, which absorbs red and blue light, *not* green. We see all the greens scattered, filling the air with a huge exhalation of color, and identify nature by its signature of loss: green. So, ironically, the colors we relish happen in the mind, not in the world. Apples are everything *but* red—when light hits them, only the red rays are reflected into our eyes, and we think: *That's red!*

On other planets, organisms would adapt to the brew of

light emitted by their own type of star, filtered by their own tailor-made atmosphere. Hotter stars, for instance, give off more blue light. It might be fun living in a blue-hued nature, unless the sky were blue, too, which could leave one in a muddle, unless one evolved to gauge the subtle differences. Photosynthesis is so successful on Earth it's likely to power life elsewhere. Red dwarfs (the most common stars) emit less visible light than our sun and vegetation on their planets might photosynthesize in black to make the most of low light by absorbing all colors. We, too, have adapted to our sun's dialect of light. Florida is a land where the leaves are those in paintings by Goya: dark lugubrious greens. Pale greens would fry in the sun, so the glossy leaves of the hibiscus, palm, and fig use a reddish-green pigment as sunscreen (it wicks away extra sunlight).

In Northern winters, the branch tips of blue spruce look glazed with ice when they're flushed with new growth, a blue so startling the tree goes by its name. Thinking of colors we identify with nature—*avocado, sea foam, mint, turquoise*—I wonder how we missed *blue fir*, a shade of talcy blue that hovers close to light green. Many languages don't distinguish between blue and green at all. The Japanese regard our green traffic signals as blue, for instance, while to the Vietnamese both sky and leaves are a green-blue they can refine as *sky* green-blue or *leaf* green-blue. As late as the turn of the twentieth century, the Swedes were using the same word for blue and black, and although at first that seems horribly limiting, and maybe even morose (unless you think of black as a shade of blue), it would have spurred wonderful imagery as people sought ways to specify exactly the shade of blue they meant. Was it jay blue, sapphire blue, wild-lupine blue, window-cleaner blue, denim blue, neon blue, open-water blue, chicory blue, ultramarine, indigo, periwinkle, or the blue shadow at the bottom of a hole you dig in the snow? In contrast, Russians and Italians see light blue as a separate color from dark blue, just as we call light red *pink*. Welsh poets say *yng nglas y dydd*, "in the blue of the day," when referring to dawn, and also use *glas* (blue) as a symbol for birth and death. In their lyrical trust not only does day and life dawn, so does death when one dawns on the other side.

On our planet, green, blue, and red seem to dominate— the blue skies and ocean, of course, the greens of leaves, and reds so sense-stirring we're bowled over by them. The redder the sunrise or sunset the more it thrills us. The color of blood and fire, red excites the eye. When a man sees bright red (battle uniform, say, or a red-hot mama in a slinky red dress), his adrenal gland secretes more adrenaline to tune his body for trouble. In lab studies, red triggers the release of the hormone epinephrine, and blood pressure increases, the pulse speeds up, breathing quickens, and perspiration follows. The body instinctively treats red as an aggressive color, a cue for arousal and energy. No one can stay calm long in an endlessly eye-catching red room. Coca-Cola, Campbell's soup, Colgate toothpaste, and countless other companies flash red in their packaging to entice customers. It's small wonder the word *red* sashays through our language. Anger us and we *see red*. An unfaithful woman is branded with a *scarlet* letter. In *red-light districts* people buy carnal pleasures. We like to celebrate *red-letter days* and *roll out the red carpet*, while trying to avoid *red tape*, *red herrings*, and *being in the red*. We carry the color red in our veins, we are soft sacs of a red liquid. Spill a little of it and women produce life. Spill a lot and we die. And that's just us; other creatures perceive red in differently fascinating ways.

At the moment, I'm savoring a fluorescent red sunrise

whose sienna fleece contrasts strikingly with pale pink banners. A scarlet male cardinal has landed on a palm leaf. His
dusky mate, perching in a nearby hedge, is not so eye-catching.
To us, that is. Other cardinals find her perfectly red, especially
when she flirts by puffing up and shivering like a baby bird.
Were there baboons in the street, the females would be flashing
red netherparts. Not all mammals see red as I do. Cats live in
a black, white, and gray world, one I can glimpse. Since only
the cone cells of our eyes sense color, and they're concentrated
in the center, everything I see *out of the corner of my eye* is
colorless. That part of my retina views the world in cat-like
monochrome. A folder propped up beside me is a gray blur until
I turn my head and center it: green cardboard filled with white
notebook pages written on in black, flagged with bright yellow
Post-its, on one of which the word *leeches* has been scrawled
in green ink. Color-blind people, like Operation Migration's
whooping crane guide Bill Lishman, have trouble telling red
from green—a lucky break for the cranes since, as a boy, Lishman had planned on piloting planes in the Royal Canadian
Cadets, who turned him down because, by global agreement,
red and green runway lights guide pilots, and planes flash a red
light on the left wing, green on the right.

Male and female barn swallows, cedar waxwings, and most
of the world's songbirds appear the same color to me, but they
see beyond me into the realm where plumage reflects ultravio-
let light and flowers are decorated with to-us-invisible targets
and landing pads—for birds see more colors than we do and
read much finer distinctions among them.

In nature, flashy dress usually signifies sex or danger. Arrow-
poison frogs warn in screaming colors: *Don't touch!* Monarch
butterflies, heart-stoppingly beautiful with their digitalis-like

poison, signal: *Don't eat!* Banded bumblebees warn of stingers, diamond-backed rattlers of venom, with colors that proclaim: *Dangerous if attacked or eaten!* Even plants read and respond to color. When tomato plants are exposed to far-red, well beyond human vision, they react as if they were racing rivals and spiral high, boost the chlorophyll and protein in their leaves, and fruit earlier than their neighbors.

In the days before synthetic colors, some red dye came from such plant sources as henna, madder, or archil, and others from insects like *Laccifer lacca*, excellent for lacquering or shellacking wood. But competitive dyers also sought a *perfect* red, by which they meant commercially perfect: stable, easily absorbed by fabric, and resistant to fading.

When Cortés galloped into Mexico as a four-legged god, he discovered that the emperor, Montezuma, claimed the right to wear a resplendent solar red, and imposed on his subjects a special tax to be paid in cochineal insects, from which the vibrant dye came. The Spanish quickly monopolized the world's supply of cochineal, which became both high-status and expensive. In 1587 alone, the Spanish shipped sixty-five tons of it home. Other countries coveted it, pirated shipments from Spanish galleons, and tried to raise it cheaply in their own colonies. The equivalent of corporate espionage ensued.

Much as they loved the luxe red, people tried like the dickens to unpuzzle the dye, without success. For the longest time they couldn't even agree if it was plant or animal. In an era of poor microscopes, cochineal's secrets simply defied scrutiny, and as a result it spawned recklessly high bets and lots of controversy. As it turns out, cochineal is a fragile little beetle, related to scale, that lives on the prickly pear cactus.

The female produces carminic acid for defense against ants and the like, and she's pure red. Pinch her and she bleeds a red so fierce it gives cloth a dye that can outlast empires. Male and female differ wildly in this species, and that added to the confusion, with rumors of angelic inseminators. The flightless females crawl around prickly pear cactus, waiting for their "flying husbands" to descend. After that, alas, they're engorged with a pure red precious to European hominids, at times more craven than a cadre of ants.

Why not set up cochineal colonies in Europe? Cochineal is notoriously hard to ranch. For centuries, Mexicans enjoyed success by hand-rearing small numbers, which they were able to breed for size and color, until they arrived at a robust new species twice as large as wild cochineal. Even so, cochineal insects were sensitive to weather, and it took seventy thousand dried insects to produce one pound of red dye. In the days before synthetic dyes, the more European monarchs and gentry wore the fashionable scarlet red, the more cochineal figured in society and fed or bled the economy.

Most often we see red as decorative, not purposeful, not exploitable. But color is mainly trickery, much of it designed by clever plants to waylay a potential pollinator, or used by animals to scare away a predator or share important (often life-and-death) information. Like other life-forms, we unknowingly employ red to signal our intentions or moods. An emotional octopus changes color, glowering red when angry; we blush red when embarrassed. Like the hummingbird and the tomato plant, we're passionate about red, a blood color that excites our senses, sometimes into fright, but most often into arousal. Like other animals, we tell time in part by the color of the sky, and follow color as a feeding guide, to detect ripe fruit, edible plants, and fresh game. We even use color for spiritual nourishment.

At dawn in India on the spring equinox, as a priest with red-stained skin chants, an excited crowd tosses clouds of red powder into the air, symbolizing pollen, showering everyone in crimson. Elsewhere at dawn, church cardinals are donning red robes, women applying red lipstick, workmen planting red stop signs, lawyers and politicians knotting red "power ties" around their necks before they enter the scorching fray.

TIME RACES DAWN'S MANY FACES

~

Absence makes the heart grow fonder,
Isle of Beauty, fare thee well!

—THOMAS HAYNES BAYLY

At the west end of Sunrise Avenue sits a grand old tan wedding-cake hotel, lined with sugar-cube-shaped topiary trees. While the rising sun washes its aging face with soft yellow light, the blinds rise halfway up most windows, like sleepy eyelids, as the inhabitants, waking, take only a small swig of their local star. After breakfast is time enough for the whole molten inferno.

A hard rain last night and lots of yesterday washed the surface of the city and filled countless thimble- and pocket-sized nooks for animals to drink from, and also *slaked* the plants' thirst. Love that Biblical word. Blowing slantwise, rain bounced off car roofs and slid down rear windows in a flow of large tears. Tears from a local shrine: Our Lady of Mercedes. The gray trunks of royal palms, spackled with lichen in a fashionable shade of green usually named *sea foam* or *moss*, look even more like a Jackson Pollock painting when the rain has washed away the sand and salt that blows two blocks from the sea. Local women get salt-glow rubs, and the streets do, too. Sometimes it seems like everything alive lives in a perpetual scrub and slough of old skin.

So many parts of the planet wait for their rainy season through devastating drought months. Here, in southern Florida, the downpours are accompanied by 90-degree days, which addles the tourist birds, signaling both a changing season and migration time, when fine-feathered humans depart in small flocks.

By the end of April, the cafés on Poinciana Boulevard are nearly empty, and six months' worth of street disemboweling begins with backhoes, cherry pickers, random sounds of concrete dropped from a great height onto planks, and the pickling beep of heavy machinery in reverse. More tunes for the mockingbirds. Birdsong continues as if nothing out of the ordinary were occurring, nothing as frightening, say, as a thunderstorm, even though these sounds clang against the body like constant artillery. Even the frailest human or Chihuahua seems to take it all in stride.

A clean well-groomed pug walks by with its owner on a leash—the owner wearing a polo shirt and shorts, the pug bare-ass naked with a skinny tail curled up, exposing a star-shaped anus. As the sun rises higher, the royal palms cast shadows fifty feet long in natural sundials. Whatever catches the Midas sun's gaze turns to gold for a brief moment of pure illumination and onstage pizzazz. A second later it becomes dull, flat, unexceptional again, out of the limelight as the glow moves to some new star.

A familiar workman crosses the street holding a cup of coffee at waist level in his right hand and a bag of breakfast

buns in his left. He never varies. I presume as he walks from
parking lot to hotel he sees me two stories up, like a sphinx
facing the sunrise, partly visible through the stucco railing,
mug beside me on a white wicker table, my sleep-tousled hair
levitating in the breeze.

A man I recognize as a neighbor walks by briskly, carrying
a small bag. Shadows climb his chest until he's across from me,
striding into pure sunlight, then, as he passes, his shadow trails
behind him. Shaggy-haired with a soup-strainer mustache, he
looks like a sloth, that strange slow-motion eponymous creature
with two or three toes, which lives its life atop a single tree,
down which it shimmies once a week to defecate at the base
of its tree, thus fertilizing it, in a rather creative exchange of
goods and services. Because a sloth moves so slowly, a complete
ecosystem of bugs, bacteria, and other bionts lives in its fur. For
all I know, the hairy man might be giving asylum to an equal
number of freeloaders. I hear we carry two to five pounds of live
bacteria around with us, in our own private ecosystems of flora
and fauna, some mischief-makers, some harmless vagabonds.
My neighbor takes his bacteria for a stroll at the same time
every morning, presumably going to a café for breakfast.

Two more deeply tanned workmen arrive in a glossy white
van, park in front of a restaurant, and climb out carrying coffee.
Both the coffee and their breath make small clouds in the cold.
They walk inside and return a moment later into a dawn now
the powder blue of nursery walls, open the van's twin doors, and
begin removing a long ladder which makes the unique sound
of all metal ladders being pulled, rung by rung, from trucks. I
laugh, glance away to focus only on the sound. *Ladder, ladder,*
I say silently in my mind, pronouncing each syllable slowly as
the rattle-clank-scrape-gong-clatter of rungs continues.

Then I sit down to breakfast—one needs to be fortified for all the noise to come in this noisy city, coast, culture. I don't mean natural noises like the nightly booming of the black drum fish in the canals, whose loud mating calls invade houses and seem to torture the residents (all black drums do is use a sonic muscle to vibrate a swim bladder, but the sound carries through water, soil, and walls). This rackety island runs the gamut from mildly strident human hullabaloo to a long earsplitting Niagara of empty bottles crashing from restaurant dumpsters into waiting garbage trucks.

High winds off the sea herd the clouds away, and spin hairstyles into small private medusas. The palm fronds hula, and the doves face into the wind lest, feathers ruffled, they take flight against their will. A white-hot dawn cha-chas with birdcalls, and then the first growling car dominates the soundscape. The first bus lumbers to a stop with pig-squealing brakes, the first delivery trucks make *Stand clear!* pings as they creep in reverse. The unmistakable sound of heavy wooden planks being dropped from about five feet is enough to rouse any slugabed, bird or beast. All are animal sounds, theirs and ours.

The bus moans as it changes gears. How confusing the downshift arpeggio must be to other animals. Or do they file the noise as one human sound among so many? If there were an Audubon field guide to humans, what calls, songs, alarms, contact sounds would it include? The courtship and mating habits, the nests we construct, the ceremonies and brooding would fill thousands of pages. Even the sounds of the other meaning of *brooding*, when the mind creates worries and nurtures them like African violets.

The growling of mastodons in the distance I recognize as human garbage and recycling truck noises. I haven't a

clue what the birds and lizards make of their clangor, except
to identify them as human, more of our natural sounds. Or
maybe they construe the sound as truckish: armored giants
uttering their own elephantine version of *Hi, Joe.* What do
they make of the stoplights' bright plumage? Do they realize
the red, yellow, green flashes belong to the human part of their
landscape? I presume they regard the terrain of cities as just
another niche, one of so many on this planet where they may
roost, flock, breed, raise their young.

Sometimes there's enough hullabaloo for a pagan festival,
and the time of year is right: Imbolc on the Neolithic calendar,
halfway between the winter solstice and the spring equinox,
when fire and purification of the spirit were required at dawn
to ensure spring lambs and the increasing ardor of the sun. It's
a holiday dedicated to the pagan goddess Brigit (later changed
to St. Brigid), a day of poetry and divination.

A nesting sparrow, perched on a drain spout with one toe
curled over the edge, warbles, then hushes, and a moment later
soars to another high point in the ramparts of its morning.
Nesting season overlaps nicely with Imbolc, because according
to folklore, the hag goddess is supposed to change into a bird
on Imbolc and fly around, gathering enough firewood for the
last cold months and carrying them skyward in her beak.

Three blocks away, Sunrise Avenue encounters a pale pre-
monition of sun nearly hidden behind a white stucco wall that
divides someone's beach from his neighbor's. As far as I can
tell, there are no lines in the sand, but a great many NO TRES-
PASSING and PRIVATE PROPERTY signs, cement walls, and locked
gates. Who can measure and control his piece of ocean? Who
can teach her sands to mind her on a windy beach? When the
sun rises high enough to shower light onto the land, the air

becomes visible because it's full of water vapor and blowing sand, and both, though minute, are large enough to scatter light. For a short magical spell the invisible looms, solid as glass rain, then vanishes again.

A tiny gecko hugging the stucco wall inflates a red balloon on its throat. In contrast, the larger local lizards prefer pavement-walking to wall-climbing. Like the birds, they're used to the flocks of humans and their toys, and one will dally at the edge of the sidewalk until you stop, bend over, and peer down, casting the tiny lizard in shade. Then it will cock its head, roll an eye up at you, hesitate a moment longer, and dart from sight faster than human eye can follow. Green anoles cross the pavement in small jagged dashes, pausing and hesitating several times en route. The motion is Chaplinesque, and they're easy to picture with cane, bowler hat, and spats. Large curly-tailed geckos do push-ups on porch steps to impress would-be mates.

Will the curly-tailed geckos still be here next year, the green anoles and ghost ants and boat-tailed grackles and troubadour mockingbirds that take flight with a flash of white on each wing? How will the scented reality of this Floridian season nest in my memory? It's odd that we think of memory only in terms of the past, when we remember backward, forward, sideways, and right now. A pattern-mad supposing machine, the brain just makes a best guess at things, over and over, based on memory and a convenient sense of time. Much of our life is spent living by seasonal time, not mere chronicity, as we wait for nature to go about its normal ways. There are long pastures of calm, broken suddenly by the indelible thrill of seeing a crane or sharing a kiss, and then the long hours afterward, as the excitement mellows. Of course, we also live by chronicity.

One of the most curious and uncanny things that humans do is shifting allegiance between those two perceptions of time.

How fitting that my wristwatch broke yesterday. The sense of time it keeps is merely, though ingeniously, human. The brain pictures time as a commodity that can be spent, saved, wasted. The brain pictures time as motion, something that "waits for no man," when in reality it's we who are moving and changing, and time stationary.

Without trying, and against my conscious wishes even, my brain's shopkeepers tell time, in part, by the timetables of all these neighbors, the arrival of workmen, the chiming of church bells, the birdsong and anole skittering, the opening of stores, the silent bulldozers at noon, the congestion of cars after work, and the sounds of showers and radios from behind closed doors. We time our conduct and monitor one another. Other animals also have errands to run and appointments to keep, but they don't juggle many things at once. I've made a to-do list for our migration back north, and also a list of items I'm leaving here in Florida in storage. Other animals store things, but only humans store information outside of their brains. Only humans make long personal lists that intersect with other people's long lists, and find both relief and insidious glee in checking them off when done. On such occasions, we seem to steer time. Then, as minor potentates, we can begin and end things, a mastery rare enough to thrill.

At last the sun pokes its hot face around the corner of the building, and when I look at it directly it flashbulbs into my eyes. There's little foot traffic, since it's Sunday morning, and daylight savings time at that. This means I'll find the sun up later for a spell, and it will light the sky longer—until well after dinner.

Unfortunately, my body's internal rhythms can't be reset that easily. Following the sun, they stay in synchrony with nature as the seasons change, and despite my work or wake schedule, remain on standard time. Not a problem when they're released from daylight savings time in autumn, but a real bugbear in spring. That one-hour difference is enough to disturb a host of physiological cycles for me and about 1.6 billion other people. It's only one hour's difference, but it translates into ten weeks of a skewed relationship between waking and dawn. But natural light doesn't seem to matter as much to us now, since people tend to decide bedtime according to work and television broadcast schedules. When people resettle in different time zones, they even revise their bedtimes so that they can watch the same TV shows.

Clocks define the morning for most people, and few wake to birdsong or watch the sunrise anymore. Instead, they may be jolted from sleep by a predatory alarm clock, bolt down a cup of tea or coffee as fuel (my dad used to request his decaf coffee "unleaded"), and tune in to the newspaper, TV, or radio, where news is served up as crime, war, politics, or disaster. I know some people who rue the morning because it means work or school, and others who greet the light with special prayers or meditations. Like many artists, and mystics too, I prize dawn's half-open doorway between dream and wakefulness, when any thought is possible. I don't think of it as a time of loss but as a kind of freedom, a chance to tangle with life once more.

The silvery sun warms the flesh, a thin gauze of fog drifts across the ocean, and the sky opens into a flawless, endless pale blue. Then a flotilla of fluffy clouds races overhead, just above the parapets and steeples of my Moorish building, creating a powerful optical illusion—the looming edifice is in motion, not the clouds, and I am being carried along in its wake.

After Earth rolls in its sleep twice more, a huge weighty event we nickname *two days*, I'll find dawn light rising in my own garden. The bulbs will be starting to open, their leaves the pale new green of spring, and the treetops flushed dusty rose with new buds. In an alternate reality, many miles away, lives my home with all its flora and fauna. Because I have sensed it—touched, inhaled, seen it—it exists as a renewable memory.

SUMMER

ITHACA, NEW YORK

DANGEROUS DAWN

A DARTING MOTION ATOP THE TREE catches my eye. Moving fast as a ghost ant, it's much larger and less linear—a hummingbird! What is it doing back so early? The thermometer reads only 48 degrees—too cold for bee or sphinx moth. But not for the little inferno inside a hummingbird's chest. Still, many hummingbirds do die in their sleep. Swiveling at high speed among thousands of blossoms, hummingbirds devour high-octane nectar to fuel their flights. They must eat every fifteen minutes or so because they burn life at a fever pitch, with tiny hearts drumrolling at 500 beats per minute. That leaves them dangerously exhausted, and at day's end they enter a metabolic limbo, when breathing grows shallow and the heart slows. What a struggle to restart their racing engines on a chilly dawn. Waking up becomes a death-defying act. But most, like the red-bibbed gent at my window, survive. Somewhere his iridescent female may be guarding a nest no larger than an egg cup. As he chases a bothersome wasp away, I can imagine the confusion of the European explorers who spotted hummingbirds for the first time on our shores and thought they were colossal bees.

Many of us also die in our sleep. Then, instead of one day opening, all the days close. Why is dawn so dangerous? Blood pressure rises to rouse a body from sleep, and morning blood vessels also become less elastic. Stretched, the brittle tubes can rupture. Waking, we balance on a tightrope between sleep and awareness, trailing clouds of dreams, body aflame from the rapidly escalating stress hormone cortisol, because it takes a real jolt to rally one's senses and live again after such a long dullness. Cortisol and other hormones create the "dawn phenomenon"—blood glucose levels rise between 4:00 a.m. and 11:00 a.m., a good jump start for most of us, but not helpful for diabetics.

Sunrise gently alarms the brain, even with eyes closed, conducts the circadian rhythm section of the body and helps to orchestrate well-being. A pioneer of integrative medicine, Dr. Andrew Weil, tells of a Japanese friend diagnosed with kidney cancer:

> Upon returning home following surgery and chemotherapy, Shin Terayama found the morning unbearably beautiful and felt a great desire within to observe the sun rise from his apartment rooftop. When it rose he felt a ray enter his chest, sending energy through his body. "I felt something wonderful was going to happen. . . . I was just so happy to be alive," he says. This experience inspired Shin to change his diet and improve his lifestyle as well as to perform the daily ritual of watching the sunrise—the one thing he looked forward to each day. The sun ray penetrating his chest on his Tokyo

rooftop became symbolic of a psychospiritual transformation that connected him to a larger kind of energy and initiated his own healing process.

There's a reason the early bird catches the worm. Sleeping animals are clueless and guileless; predators do their best work at dawn. Humans, too, often prefer to silence a sleeping enemy and wage important battles at dawn. The Sun Salutation in yoga first began as worship to the Hindu solar deity Surya, a god with golden arms and hair who races across the dawn sky in a chariot pulled by seven horses, representing the seven colors of the rainbow. On the battlefield, ancient heroes sang hymns to Surya at daybreak, asking for strength to subdue foes throughout the day.

Duels are traditionally fought at dawn, no doubt because rivals are less likely to damage each other in dim light when they're sleepy—especially if they're forced to walk away from each other, then turn quickly and fire before they have chance to aim. It seems fitting the word *duel* is a contraction of the Latin words *duo* and *bellum* ("two" and "war"), since a duel is war contracted to the bare minimum: just two foes. It's usually begun by a dishonored man slapping his rival across the cheek and loudly demanding: "Pistols at dawn!"

The faith of early rising is that one has awakened aboveground, and that the night-damp and dreamy confusion will be baked solid by the rising sun. In English we use the word *wake* for such different realities: ceasing to sleep, holding a vigil or party beside someone who has died, a disturbance in the water after a ship passes, or the aftermath or consequence of anything. They all meet in a past nearly beyond imagining, in the Old Norse word *vaka*, "an opening in the ice." That opening could lead to fish, hunting, travel, driftwood for ship repair, suicide, or just a badly needed escape from the cage of long winters.

In Swahili, wishing someone a good night translates as "Wake up living," grim humor to be sure. In one sense, to wake is to survive a small death, one of perhaps 31,025, spaced out every sixteen hours or so over the arc of a longish life. That's scary enough to give kids nightmares, especially if, beforehand, they say the bedtime prayer that includes imminent death as a real possibility: "If I should die before I wake, I pray the Lord my soul to take." It's telling, I suppose, that in English we name our bad dreams *nightmares*, as if they were female horses galloping out of control, or *mares*, the pockmarked craters of the Moon. Yet we haven't needed a separate word for fabulous dreams, delicious dreams, dreams of blessed calm. The Bantu have, calling their blissful dreams *bilita mpatshi* (pronounced bee-LEE-tah mm-POT-she). We could also use an equivalent of the Indonesian *Kekau*, the feeling of waking from a horrible nightmare, still slightly tippy but glad to step onto shore once again.

IN THE SPIRIT OF
SEI SHŌNAGON

A WOMAN WHO DISCOVERED DAWN'S spell at an early
age was poetic, opinionated, high-spirited Sei Shōnagon
(tenth century), whose famous *Pillow Book* opens with this
appreciation: "In spring, the dawn is the most beautiful time of
day. As the light creeps over the hills, their outlines are dyed a
faint red and wisps of purplish cloud trail over them." Another
day, lowering her ink-fattened pen to the paper, she wrote: "In
winter, the early morning . . . waking to see everything glazed
in frost. . . . Servants hustle from room to room, bringing coal
and stirring up the drowsy embers in the braziers. But it gets
warmer as the sun rises in the sky and the servants stop tending
the braziers. When the ashes snuff out the last of the embers,
this is dreadfully boring."

In matters of the heart, she also chronicled the dawn,
noting the voluptuous delicacies of waking before a lover, or
watching him dress to steal away unnoticed (they both hoped).
The walls were paper, intimacies whispered. "In the winter,"

she wrote, "when it is very cold and one lies buried under the bedclothes listening to one's lover's endearments, it is delightful to hear the booming of a temple gong, which seems to come from the bottom of a deep well. The first cry of the birds, whose beaks are still tucked under their wings, is also strange and muffled. Then one bird after another takes up the call. How pleasant it is to lie there listening as sound becomes clearer and clearer!"

Sei Shōnagon wasn't her real name, but her station, and how she was addressed in the palace, where Sei derived from her clan's name (Kiyohara) and Shōnagon meant "minor counselor," which would have referred to a male relative. Upper-class women, though often powerful in their own way, existed legally as ripples in a male-centered society. I'm sure she had a more personal name and also a pet name. I wish I knew what friends called her, but scholars have been debating her true name for over a thousand years, guessing that quite possibly it was Kiyohara Nagiko, who was the daughter and granddaughter of two well-known poets—Kiyohara no Motosuke and Kiyohara no Fukayabu—middle-ranking courtiers who didn't acquire much money or power, but were able to place her at court.

Little is known about Sei except that she was born in Japan in around 966, and became lady-in-waiting to teenage empress Sadako when Sei was a divorced woman of twenty-seven. She adored the young ethereal empress, whose favorite she soon became, and her palace life mainly included amusing the young emperor and empress (political decisions were made by a regent), helping with many of their elaborate rituals, writing and reciting clever poems, taking pilgrimages and other trips, and having affairs. Many courtiers, servants, tradesmen, monks, messengers, and visitors completed the sprawling household's endless dramas—most of which were public, simply because of the architecture.

The palace was a single-story wooden building with verandas, and very little privacy since the rooms used fabric for walls. Branching arms housed many small bedrooms or led to outlying wooden buildings, exquisitely manicured gardens, and a lotus pond. Sei's boudoir was framed by a rail around the top, from which hung curtains, hiding her from view, since it was indelicate for aristocratic ladies to reveal themselves to passersby. But she could at least overhear the tantalizing goings-on, and swap short poems with lovers, who crept in at nightfall and stole away at dawn. Then she promptly wrote poems in the afterglow or—often—pique. Her tiny room probably held a grass mat and blankets, table, brazier, basin, and clothes chests. In these chilly quarters whose walls breathed and fluttered in all weather, people wore layers of long, colorful flowing robes, tunics, and pants.

One day the empress received a gift of beautiful notebooks, which she planned to discard. Sei asked if she might have them to make one of the era's hard pillows, and thus she received the miscellany of blank notebooks which became known as *The Pillow Book*. On those pages, she chronicled the intrigues of court, her thoughts, observations of nature, anecdotes, character sketches, poems, diary notes, and 164 remarkable lists with such headings as *Things That Irritate Me* ("Just as a woman is about to tell me something really interesting, and I'm sitting there just dying to hear it, her baby starts crying!"), *Things That Have No Redeeming Qualities* ("Ugly people with disagreeable personalities"), *Things That Look Hot and Uncomfortable* ("Fat people with hair plastered against their foreheads"), *Scruffy Things* ("The inside of a cat's ear"), *Things That Are the Reverse of Each Other* ("The feeling I have seeing a man I once loved but don't anymore"), *Things That Make Me Happy* ("I am delighted when I can fit together the scraps of a letter someone discarded and then read it!"). Here is *Things That Give a Clean Feeling*:

> An earthen cup.
> A rush mat.
> A new metal bowl.
> The play of the light on water as
>   one pours it into a vessel.
> A new wooden chest.

I can see her now, kneeling at a low table, as she rolls up the filmy sleeves of her tunic and reaches for a brush lying across the edge of an inkstone. Lifting it with thin steady fingers, she dips the brush into the ink, tip first, then cheeks, and waits for the bristles to drink and swell. Rolling the brush lightly against the rim of the inkstone, she wipes away the excess and settles it onto the piece of paper in front of her, then swiftly moves it across the page, watching the brush stretch and breathe like a small live sable.

Social fashion decreed that at dawn, after a lover crept away and hurried home, he immediately wrote his sweetheart a poem of twenty-three syllables, which a messenger would deliver. The lady was obliged to compose a poem immediately in reply. And so Sei, a mischievous, snobby, and promiscuous poet of recognized talent, wrote and received many amorous aubades. She also wrote prose about lovers, what rituals she expected of them, and how they should act at dawn, taking pains to ridicule fools, celebrate romantics, and reveal her impish sense of humor. She concludes that a good lover should "behave as elegantly at dawn as at any other time," which means:

> He drags himself out of bed with a look of dismay on his face. The lady urges him on: "Come, my friend, it's getting light. You don't want anyone to find you here." He gives a deep sigh as if to say that the night has not been nearly long enough and that it's agony to leave. Once up, he does not instantly pull on his trousers. Instead he comes close to the lady and whispers whatever was left unsaid during the night. Even when he is dressed, he still lingers, vaguely pretending to be fastening his sash.
>
> Presently, he raises the lattice, and the two lovers stand together by the side door while he tells her how he dreads the coming day, which will keep them apart; then he slips away. . . . This moment of parting will remain among her most charming memories.
>
> Indeed, one's attachment to a man depends largely on the elegance of his leave-taking. If he jumps out of bed, scurries about the room, tightly fastens his trouser-sash, rolls up the sleeves of his Court cloak, over-robe, or hunting costume, stuffs his belongings into the breast of his robe and then briskly secures the outer sash—one really begins to hate him.

Well received at court during her lifetime, her *Pillow Book* has remained a classic ever since, and the recognized precursor to the literary genre known as *saijiki*, literally "a year's journal," in which the author blends observations of the natural world with personal experience. Another heir to *The Pillow Book* is the Japanese genre known as *zuihitsu*, literally "following the will of the pen," or "the pen following the mind," short prose that touches on miscellaneous subjects. American abstract painter Robert Motherwell said he followed the will of his brush in a similar way, because "in the brush doing what it's doing, it will stumble on what one couldn't do by oneself." The *zuihitsu* isn't as loose or meandering as stream of consciousness, but less single-minded than a formal essay. It wanders as our thoughts do, not freely but following related pathways.

In English, the word *wander* is only a vowel away from *wonder*, though it can be a complete rhyme when spoken by a Southerner. The two words also blur in the mind, where it takes a fresh eye to see the familiar, and if you wander just a little from the habitual you may stumble on the truly wondrous. For example, if I weren't paying attention to the dawn on purpose this morning, I would have missed how slanting light hit the creek water near my house, revealing the shadows of a colony of water striders, insects that skim along on the surface tension of water. They were communicating through ripples, tapping a Morse code of desire—the frenzied males at 90 times a minute, the females only 10 times a minute. Striders are tiny oarsmen hard to spot at the best of times, but the low sun magnified their shadows on the bottom of the creek, their footpads stood out, and they looked like an array of sliding dominoes. At such moments, time suddenly snags on a simple *Wow!*

Another eye-snag: a large plump rabbit loping by. When I migrate as far as from Florida to New York, I have to retrain my eye. All my senses, really. The scent of morning tea, for instance—jasmine pearls: green tea wrapped up tight with jasmine—reminds me of the jasmine hedges in Florida. Here I can stroll beside viburnum and lilac hedges, equally pungent, but different narcotic scents.

Last night the "dog-days" cicadas skirled loud as Scottish infantry, piping their whereabouts and mood across the woods. These are annual visitors, invisible night screechers with red eyes who somehow manage to synchronize their calls, the vocal equivalent of circling doves. Every seventeen years, their cousins, the "periodic" cicadas, rise from the soil like zombies, holding clear orange-veined wings tent-like over their bodies, filling the sky with their tinny love and turf calls, climbing the screen doors, and blanketing the ground with casings and carcasses. Connecting the loudness of the adults to the silence of the nymphs, Chinese folk medicine prescribes cicada casings for ear infections, or to quiet a crying baby. Some local Indian tribes enjoyed the dog-days cicadas as food, frying the popcorn-like nymphs in butter, but regarded periodic cicadas as portents of evil. Why seventeen-year cycles? They're all teens, all adolescents ripe for sex. Appearing only once every seventeen years is a perfect evolutionary strategy—what predator could wait that long or arrive at exactly the same time?

In 1689, Sei Shōnagon's countryman Matsuo Bashō wrote in his haiku journal *The Narrow Road to the Interior*:

Serenity and yet
Penetrating the rock
The voice of the cicada

Bashō composed another haiku about cicadas the following summer:

So soon to die
You can hardly tell it
By the cicada's voice

In haikus, one often finds cicadas molting, usually linked with the theme of impermanence, that form is emptiness, emptiness form, and life on earth only vanity and illusion. It's an ancient poignancy, a symbol that arose long before Buddhism, one of the soul releasing its earthly hull.

I wish I could share these local sights and sounds with Sei Shōnagon, who prized "the clear voice of cicadas," and "men who recite poetry on horseback," and how "when crossing a river in bright moonlight, the water scatters in showers of crystal under the oxen's feet." She also loved the simple, self-renewing surprise of morning, when the world appears like a magic trick. "At dawn," she writes, "one wakes up with a start and sees that it is daytime—most astonishing."

DAWN IN THE GARDEN OF
COSMIC REFLECTION

~

WHERE IS THE BEST PLACE to find the sunrise in a land of lakes and gorges? I like watching the sun seep around the base of woodland trees or rise over the lake, especially since there is no "sea level" for many miles. Our long cold lake churns a mile wide and hundreds of feet deep. Once it was glacier, and the land around it retains that frigid aura. It's hard to grasp the unimaginably slow chiseling of water on rock that created this jagged landscape. My little Eden sits high above an invisible sea, where the rising sun has just chosen the flank of an old sycamore in the front yard and oiled its peeling bark with a soft golden light.

Despite the floral luxuriance now, this past winter was a killer which included some of the coldest days on record. Like other gardeners, I lost plants that had bloomed so long and robustly they'd become friends of mine, and I had to rebuild beds I'd spent years growing. I used to have ferns and raspberry bushes, which died in the winter cold, and that hit me hard because they were reminders of my childhood home in Pennsylvania, where my dad raised raspberries, and shared his bushes with me when I first moved to Ithaca. My mother donated some of her fiddlehead ferns. A garden often contains personal histories and mementos, living pages of a life. How does one protect oneself against such loss, not only the loss of plants but the loss of the memories they enshrined? When Ari, an ancient mystic, went walking through his woods he saw the trees filled with familiar souls calling and singing among the leaves.

Light laddering up the trees leads the eye smoothly from ground to sky, where our gods and our dead loved ones live, bridging the mineral earth with the breathless blue unknown of space and all that's beyond our power and ken. Trees offer refreshment in summer: their leaves are tiny fountains misting and cooling the air. Of all the trees in my backyard—sleek, fir, fruited, or evergreen—my favorites may be the dawn redwoods, rust-colored deciduous Chinese trees thought to be the ancestors of the California sequoia. I've planted two and watched them dig in their roots, fan out stacks of thin graceful limbs, and zing toward the sky.

Imagine being planted in one spot, many-limbed, shedding, wounded here and there by a careless mower or a lean hungry squirrel who peeled back your bark to suck on sap. Imagine lofting and spreading, delicately, with the cantilevered balance that humans call "graceful." Imagine how cold the snow feels at the base of your trunk, the steady grip and weighty expanse of the earth, usually swamped with life, its drink slowed in winter when your hungry roots, ever probing and sucking, lie quiet. Imagine sensing the light without eyes, encoding the rising dawn on hard, wrinkled bark, as night shadows wash through, behind, and above the umbrella of your twigs and branches. Imagine the weight of a landing bird, the scratch of squirrel feet. Imagine bursting into bloom all over and oozing a perfume irresistible to bees and butterflies, who plunge into your petals without knowing why. Imagine the sag and decline of old limbs, slack, sprained backward, with twig tips nearly touching the ground. Imagine your calluses and scars, kinks, sites of amputation. Imagine utter rigidity, though heavy with a cavalcade of sleeping buds. Imagine the withering rustle of autumn leaves and leaf shed, your limbs growing bare, lighter, and cooler. Now imagine the tug of the breeze, and if only for a moment, and ever so slightly, creak.

How marvelous it is to be alive on a planet that produces trees that grow leafy, bloom, and broadcast scent. Also that we evolved to appreciate them. After all, we didn't need to, they don't bloom for our pleasure. Yet to revel in the senses is to merge with the rest of nature. There was a time before birth when the outside world was inseparable from oneself, when self and world were one. The body remembers that first warm darkness of the womb. At the dawn of life, before we can focus our newly opened eyes, light tells us we're separate. Alas, we can only return to that state of blended self and world by disintegrating, it's only in death that we're fully sensual. But that doesn't prevent an ecstasy of sensing while alive, among ever-expanding gardens, beginning with the invisible flora and fauna that dwell inside us, including the family we may raise, the garden we may grow, and extending out past the dawn, because Earth is a floating garden in the bell jar of space.

What started as my small backyard garden thirty years ago has bloomed into a large unruly sprawl of annuals, perennials, and cherished weeds that I scout first thing each morning, blind to most of its business and barter. In the process, the garden has become an extension of myself that I can nurture in uncommon ways—by adding mulch and rich soil, for example, instead of washing its grime away. There's something very intimate and personal about a garden—if you cherish something you pay closer attention to it and notice its ailments and curiosities, how each plant is like the others of its kind but also different in small ways. Maybe that's why a garden lends itself to such powerful metaphors, because it embodies the elemental forces of nature and includes both individuals and groups, the one and the many, facets of a life, and a staggering array of relationships. The tree flower that exudes scent, enticing bees and butterflies, grants them longer life by flavoring them with a bitter taste, shielding them from predators, which in turn allows them to travel farther, spreading the tree's pollen. I water the tree, whose roots absorb mercury from the soil, whose leaves pull carbon dioxide from the air and bestow life-giving oxygen. It even waylays beneficial insects to my garden. Tip to toe, we're part of an ancient exchange among plants and animals, a swap of goods and services.

Evolving from dawn till dusk and season to season, a garden is continuous, full of islands of color, but also constantly mutating. Something that remains the same while changing speaks to me about my personality and the personalities of others. I might only yearn for a life full of color, variety, excitement, moments of calm, and interflowing passages of shadow and light. But I can achieve that in a garden. There's something about the lavishness and restraint in a garden that appeals to me, the rampant sexuality, the blend of innocence and violence. The plants' violence, but mine too.

I may celebrate the garden, but I'm also a bringer of death, since I kill flowers when I clip them. We kill grains when we harvest them to make bread. In order to kill anything, we have to say *it's not me*, refuse to believe we share its carnival of atoms. Most often my mystical and practical sides don't war with each other quite so directly. Instead, I pause to sit on the grass and watch sphinx moth or yarrow, stroll quietly, see what's happening in nature, letting thoughts bubble up. That takes data-free time, time away from clocks, email, cell phones, computers, newspapers, televisions, radios, and all the other purveyors of information that plug us in and plug us up. A mind carries so many loads. Setting some of them down for a short spell, to loll in wonder's swaying hammock, delivers me as much now as when I was a child. So I like to spend a few rapt moments with the look and feel of an iris beard or watch the to-and-fro-ings of birds, layering new observations onto old as my eyes travel from the volatile palette of leaves to the leaves leaving in autumn.

Adding to the general tumble, I raise pretty weeds like Queen Anne's lace and verbascum, Jacob's ladder and Joe Pye weed in the beds. I always ask someone else to plant spring bulbs and not tell me where. I don't peek either. It's fun in the spring to find fritillarias poking out from behind tall, multistoried Japanese primroses, and hyacinths popping up in the oddest places. When the apple blossoms have fallen, late-blooming tulips are still shrieking with color. Sometimes a lone tulip will rise from a creeping mat of mottled lungwort. Sometimes I'll find a stray tulip shooting up from the ankle of a lilac bush. I like that about gardens—the what-is-it appearing who knows where, and if. The if factor keeps one nicely off-balance, heady one day, disappointed the next. For the most part, this laissez-faire tumble works for me, especially when I sprawl in my bay window, afloat among the taller flowers and the lower branches of the magnolia. There I can loosen my hair and sometimes feel a gentle, almost imperceptible tugging at my roots.

MATINS WITH THE NEIGHBORS
(TWO-LEGGED AND FOUR)

~

S PRING BRINGS A SPELL OF pure anticipation, when the
not-yet, the almost, the what-will-be tugs at the cells of
humans and animals alike. A howling-bright moon floats
below a coal scuttle full of stars. Soon the alarm clock of birds
begins: at 5:00 a.m., hermit thrushes in the treetops cry *Why
dontcha come to me? Here I am right near you!*, at 5:10 the robins
trill *twiddle-oo, twiddle-eedee* from the undergrowth, at 5:15 the
blackbirds *chook chook* and rattle alarm from tall trees, at 5:20
the goldfinches jibber *po-ta-to-chip* in flight, at 5:30 the female
cuckoos start bubbling chuckles in the tree crowns, at 5:40
the tanagers slur *hurry, worry, blurry, flurry* from the bushes,
at 5:50 the black-capped chickadees whistle *chik-a-dee-dee-dee*
from low branches, at 6:05 the yellow warblers blither *sweet-
sweet-sweet, little-more-sweet* from low branches, at 6:20 the blue
jays root *jay-jay-jay* from the canopies, and at 6:30 the starlings
slather a copycat medley all around.

My neighbor Georg appears while I'm on my garden rounds, and we chat about flowering weeds, beloved by his bees, and how the deer have browsed his raspberry leaves, but not the blueberry leaves. Neighbors, whose arbitrarily divided land shares a microclimate, often compare the this and that of their natural world. Spores and seeds travel freely between the properties, squirrels and other animals plant nuts and berries across the property lines. And if the deer understand that flimsy-looking humans defend their own small territories, some of which are better-tasting and more welcoming than others, they don't seem to play favorites. Within each yard, many smaller microclimates dictate the fate of hydrangea, summer sweet, or tree peony, but there are also annual trends of weather, animals, and disease.

We generalize about other animals, assume the same deer that eat daylily buds in my yard will devour his resurrection lily, standing alone and inviting near the roadway. But, like us, individual deer are fickle and have moods. One doe I've come to know is skittish and can be distracted from a succulent meal by the sound of a bicycle chain twenty yards off. Another will sit calmly chewing as I bike by, not bothering to get up, even when I circle round to look at her again. I consider her a neighbor, even if, lamentably, we can't share our insights about the green and growing world. Yesterday I saw two speckled fawns investigating a baby rabbit. Nose down, they sniffed at it, and the rabbit slowly hopped two steps forward. They followed, watching and gently sniffing, not threatening. The rabbit didn't bolt. Watching them from the round corners of its bulging black eyes, it hopped twice whenever their breath steamed close. Children tend to be curious about other young creatures, regardless of leg number; and young animals often are, too.

Claude Monet, *Rouen Cathedral, the Portal and Tour Saint-Roman. Morning Effect, White Harmony.* (RÉUNION DES MUSÉES NATIONAUX / ART RESOURCE, NEW YORK)

Aurora borealis (USAF PHOTO BY SENIOR AIRMAN JOSHUA STRANG)

False dawn or zodiacal light (DOMINIC CANTIN)

A red-veined darter covered in dew (MARTIN AMM)

Bee dusted with pollen as it collects nectar

Claude Monet, *Impression, Sunrise* (ERICH LESSING / ART RESOURCE, NEW YORK)

Katsushika Hokusai, *The Great Wave off Kanagawa* (ERICH LESSING / ART RESOURCE, NEW YORK)

Kumbh Mela festival at dawn on the banks of the Ganges River
(AMANDA MCLAUGHLIN)

Spring equinox entering an ancient temple at dawn
(KENWILLIAMS/SHADOWSANDSTONE.CCM)

Morning glory cloud, Gulf of Northern
Australia (ROB HANBURY)

Juvenile whooping cranes with costumed handlers (WWW.OPERATIONMIGRATION.ORG)

Winter sunrise in Ithaca, New York (AMY HNATKO / WWW.ASHNATKODESIGNS.COM)

Spring sunrise in Florida (CLAUDIA DOMENIG)

Tromsø, Norway, during Mørketida, in full sunlight (PER IVAR SOMBY)

Ice halo with two sun dogs, a solar column, and a solar wedge (LES COWLEY)

Two large mottled brown rabbits, grazing together in the yard, quietly eat one dandelion stalk after another, jaws moving at speed. They both follow the same routine: the rabbit breaks off the stem low down, then crunches it straight to the fluffy top. Does it like the top best, saving it for last, or does it eat it not to be wasteful? After a few stems, it sidles next to a dandelion, stretches up off its haunches, and just eats the fluff. Then it finds several more dandelions and only eats their heads, too. After a rest, it plucks stems from the bottom once more and works to the top. The second rabbit, a female, follows near and freeze-cowers if the first gets too close. Proximity makes her tense and stop feeding. Occasionally the male hops at her and away, but not really attacking or courting-dancing. I think it may be to keep her in her place. In time, he hops out of sight along a trail of dandelions, and she follows two yards behind, close enough to be a consort, far enough to feed in peace, her bulging eyes following his moves, even when she's turned away from him.

I try to imagine the tension she may feel, how it changes incrementally with his changes in posture, distance, the dangerous yet magnetic uncertainty she harbors, try to lose myself in the subtle complexities of her life. I'm using the word "feel" loosely. She's sensing nonstop and undergoing intense emotions, not thinking about them, not having *feelings*. Of course, these are only ideas about the thing, not the thing itself. I am still very much a separate being, not indivisibly rabbit for more than an instant, and only in one glade of imagining. But taking on the mental mantle of rabbit, owl, tree, slime mold, or dancing crane, however fleeting, teaches one about the amalgams of energy and chaos life forms, dissolves, forms again in new ways. I could have been like *this*: feel the follicles of hair, the twitch of furred skin, the roil of fear as a potentially dangerous and always jealous mate swings into view at the distant horizon of a curved eye that simultaneously scans the foreground and background, noting when anything first edges over the rim of awareness and begins sailing into view—a distance measurable in escape hops, provided they're fast enough. To be safe, always attend when anything changes. Freeze. Assess. Hop fast.

The yard looks different at rabbit and dandelion level, everything looms, and it's good to lower one's perspective now and then. I've never noticed before that when a dandelion goes to puffball, the seeded head rises higher than the flower so its flight won't be blocked. At dandelion level, one gets an inkling of how nature appears to a rabbit or groundhog. Or to us when we were crawling young and not as smart as a rabbit or a groundhog, our senses not yet trained by experience, our vision not yet tinted by memory.

In Celtic myth these rabbits represent Eostri, dawn goddess, hare goddess, a creature solitary, supernatural, intuitive, and fickle, and also remote and inconstant as the moon, a creature forever hopping around the sky. Woman, moon, and rabbit link through the idea of fertility and birth. Waning and rebirth, moon and rabbit fuse in the mythology of many cultures—Buddhists tell of the "hare in the moon" rather than the man, and in Egyptian hieroglyphics the rabbit is the word picture for existence itself.

Celtic calendars counted the nights, not the days, with a fortnight being half a month. The queen of the night, and the lamp of the poor, the moon kept superstition alive as she traveled around the dark thickets of the sky. She was worshiped especially during Aoruil, known as Eostur-Monath, and at the spring equinox, known as Alban (from the Latin for *white*, signifying the dawn). Eostri, the goddess of the dawn, lives even in ancient Sanskrit, where she's called Usra. From her daily rising came our words *East* and *Easter*, where the sun dawns and the son dawns again, both stepping across a threshold of light. The Germans called her Ostara and studded the hills with Easter-stones, stone altars where she was worshiped. Wherever Eostri went, a rabbit accompanied her, ensuring fertility and growth. But at the full moon, the goddess herself rose up into a great hare, a royal animal in the Celtic pantheon. The warrior queen Boudicca took a lucky hare with her into battle, where it "screamed like a woman from beneath her cloak." The fickle, powerful hare goddess ruled northern Europe for a long spell, and as Christianity borrowed from the old pagan religions, the goddess Easter became the holiday, complete with benign Easter rabbits.

Another morning, mother squirrel lopes across the yard wearing what looks like a turtleneck. It's only her baby, a squirm of fur wrapped around her neck the way squirrel moms prefer when transporting their young in this season of squirrels wearing kin. The mother's once-bushy tail, now shedding, seems too scraggy to rely on for balance. New hair will enrich it, but for the moment she's at risk because a luxuriant tail serves as counterweight, balance bar, and metronome when she's wire-walking or leaping between wobbly branches.

I like watching what squirrels do with their tails. When it rains, squirrels fold their tails up over their heads as umbrellas. As they sit and eat, they settle deep onto their haunches and throw their tails over their backs like scarves to keep warm. It's amazing the way a squirrel can clasp itself on the back with its tail, embrace and comfort itself. Humans do that, too—hug themselves when they need nurturing and no one is around—

and sometimes people rock back and forth in that pose, as if their arms belonged to another who was happy to cradle them. Tails are cozy sweaters squirrels wrap around small offspring. They fold them overhead into a sort of pompadour, to look taller when they encounter rivals. And, of course, they use them to balance like tight-rope walkers.

When a squirrel falls into the pool, as inevitably one does from time to time, I run to scoop it out with a long-handled skimmer. The pool walls are too slippery and steep for them to climb out on their own. At first, my efforts frightened them even more and it took a while to corner one, lifting it, exhausted, from the water. But through experience, and also by watching from afar, I think, the squirrels have come to know their human neighbors. Now a frantically treading squirrel will swim straight toward me, scramble onto the skimmer and wait while I lift it to ground level, then scamper away.

High above, opal-gray clouds overlap like the breast feathers of a great blue heron, a silhouette common here in the morning. Long necks tucked between their hunched shoulders and curved wings acting like airplane flaps, herons slow down to land on spindly legs. Born without the preen gland most birds use to oil their feathers, they rely on pulviplumes, special feathers with tips that crumble to a fine cleansing powder, which they comb through their regular feathers using the edge of a middle toe.

I often watch a heron fishing at the curve of creek we call Flat Rock, not far from my house—it spears fish with long pointed beak, and baits fish by shaking a foot. In Japan, the green-backed herons don't eat the bread scraps humans toss, but drop them in the water to attract fish. Some herons cleverly turn away from the sun and hunt in their own shadows. By any standard, they're savvy tool-using hunters. Two or more herons becomes a *siege* of herons, the collective term, which conjures up herons standing in the shallows and waiting patiently. It's easy to mistake their hoarse croaking for frog calls.

I've found that if I walk up to a tide pool and stand for half a minute or so, heron-like, nothing much happens. But if I stay there a little longer animals will start moving around as my shadow becomes an environmental constant and I no longer pose a threat. The same thing happens on a reef, where a good snorkeling strategy is not to cover a lot of territory, but rather find a patch of rock, hold a position over it, and wait. Herons instinctively know this strategy, or they learn it by watching the fancy footwork of their elders. I learned it from watching herons fish. But would a heron learn it by watching humans fish?

THE SOLSTICE BIRD

BIG CLUMPS OF CLOUDS ARE staggering across the night sky—giant lakes on the move. As the sky whitens to a talcy mask, the exquisite monotony of birdcalls thins to an insistent boy soprano fading into the distance. A gentle flurry of magnolia leaves guides me to where a Carolina wren, small and perfect as a Christmas ornament, begins a lavish appeal to its mate. Soon another petal flurry and she answers with the usual reply—a fluffy quiver of folded wings to melt a suitor's heart. The petal dance may not be accidental but the wren version of a fan dance; the ground beneath the tree is strewn with pink and white petals. Legend has it that Cleopatra once received Mark Antony in a bedroom a foot deep in petals.

The first long streaks of sun paint the white-barked aspens with fire, as one wren dives into a begonia pot near the front door. She and her mate have thatched a hut-shaped nest inside the hanging pot. I've read they'll roost anywhere, even in the shirt pockets of laundry on a clothesline, but I'm still startled to find the nest with four speckled cream-colored eggs one day while watering. What must the sitting wren make of the regular deluges from my watering can? Or perhaps she's used to such a weathered life. These are beautiful dawn visitors, whatever small mischief they're up to: rusty-backed, chestnut-breasted, white-throated birds with a long white eyebrow stripe. Whenever a jay or titmouse threatens, the wrens make a sound human throats can't—of a wire brush rasped across the sidewalk. Loud songster male Carolina wrens often dominate the airwaves, singing *LIB-er-ty!, CHE-wortel!, cho-WE!* while the females buzz like cicadas, a quieter and less versatile chatter. But whereas females are born with their buzz-rattle, males practice for months to memorize their song, and then they must build a repertoire. At first, they just babble nonsensical pieces of song.

Loud, insistent rasping draws me to the kitchen window to watch a strange scene unfolding. Two tufted titmice settle near the hanging begonia in the cherry tree, despite the presence of the wrens, one of which is hopping from branch to branch with a worm in its mouth, trying to get safely into the basket and feed its hours-old hatchlings. But the titmice interfere, blocking the wren's moves in what looks like a game of three-dimensional chess. All the while the other parent wren loudly rasps its wire-scratch warning. The titmice, larger gray birds with white belly and a pointed helmet-like crest of the sort soldiers often wear (presumably to look taller)—move silently, threateningly, until the wren with the worm ends up aflutter in midair, making false starts in several directions, unable to land anywhere near her young, flying at last, tired, to a high tree branch.

Then one of the titmice hops close to the basket and the

other wren dives down to chase it away—mainly by startling and harassing it. For half an hour this scene plays and replays, with one titmouse actually landing on the edge of the pot, a stab away from the chicks, before being driven off by the sound of the screen door opening, only to return a moment later. In time, the titmice leave, calling out *Peter, Peter* when they're yards apart, then locating one another in the nearby hedges with a soft one-note call of *tseep.* Suddenly they fly away in tandem. I don't know why the titmice were so menacing—I've never seen them attack the nests of other birds, never read of them feeding on hatchlings, only on worms, insects, seeds, and berries. Blue jays, on the other hand, will shoulder into a vulnerable nest and devour the young. So will raccoons. Both live nearby and frequent the rooftop and the trellis where the wrens are nesting. It's always like this in animal families, isn't it? The young are so vulnerable, so precious, and they are precious to their murderers, too, who have hungry young at home to feed.

The wren dangling a worm enters her hutch to feed one of her young. No doubt both wrens are exhausted. Carolina wrens are life mates, and when they duet, each sings a different part of what sounds like a solo song, with females adding a vibrant buzz-chord. They finish one another's sentences.

Bird of life to the druids, wrens supposedly prefer oak trees, whose soul they become. The druids regarded wrens as the king of birds, associated with divination, and celebrated them at winter solstice, the shortest day or longest night. Falling sometime between December 20 and 23 in the northern hemisphere and June 20 and 23 in the southern, solstice is the single most celebrated astronomical event on earth, a seminal dawn when the sun stands still in the sky and spring is soon to follow.

To the druids and most other peoples it symbolized rebirth on a global, local, and personal scale.

That's why on St. Stephen's Day, the day after Christmas, in Ireland, the Isle of Man, and Wales, some "wren boys" go hunting. The boys must snare a wren in the liminal hours between dawn and sunrise, emphasizing the winter solstice element and the druidical wren festival. Traditionally, they go door to door crying: "The smallest and still the king!" If they receive a coin, they give the householder a wren feather in return, which guarantees good fortune. Killing a wren at any other time of day or year brings bad luck, incurring the wrath of the druids. In Scotland the wren hunt takes place on New Year's Day, when hunters capture wrens, tie ribbons to their feet, and set them free again to beribbon the skies. According to legend, a wren betrayed St. Stephen, and so medieval theologians reviled wrens, blaming them for many bad omens. But some say the wren fell from holy favor in a conscious effort to smother any lingering druidical rites.

Very loud and resonating, the wrens in my courtyard sing WHEE-dell, tea-kettle, tea-kettle, tea-kettle. I don't know if they're feeling supernatural, elated, or just full of song.

IN THE SPIRIT OF HOKUSAI

⌒

OVER LAKE CAYUGA, A SHEEN of blackness falls away
to reveal a sun-tipped mountain capped in gold with
red light spilling down its sides. It reminds me of a famous
woodblock print, *South Wind, Clear Dawn* (popularly known
as *Red Mount Fuji at Dawn*) by the eccentric Japanese print
designer and painter Katsushika Hokusai, born in Tokyo in
1760. Hokusai changed his residence a hundred times, his name
thirty-nine times (finally choosing "the old art-crazed man"),
yet somehow spent most of his eighty-nine years creating over
thirty thousand dramatic and suggestive prints, paintings, and
books. From the age of five, he had a mania for sketching
things, "yet of all I drew prior to the age of seventy," he wrote in
his autobiography, "there is truly nothing of great note. At the
age of seventy-two I finally apprehended something of the true
quality of birds, animals, insects, fish and of the vital nature of
grasses and trees. Therefore, at eighty I shall have made some
progress, at ninety I shall have penetrated even further the

deeper meaning of things, at one hundred I shall have become truly marvelous, and at one hundred and ten, each dot, each line shall surely possess a life of its own."

It was in his seventies that he began the stunning series *Thirty-six Views of Mount Fuji*, which also includes *The Great Wave off Kanagawa*, probably the most reproduced print on earth, a scene of turbulent foam-tipped waves of cyan and pale blue clawing at three small fishing boats in which frightened men frantically bend to their oars. In the flat golden sky, billowy clouds promise a placid morning, and a tiny Mount Fuji sits calmly in the background. It's the foreground that holds all the drama, though I think most people miss the nearly capsized swift boats that carry fresh foodstuffs at dawn to the Tokyo markets from nearby villages. That the mood of the ocean and the sky don't match—galloping chariots of carnal blue under a fair-weather sky—creates a sinister beauty that alarms the senses at the same time that it reassures the psyche. To the men, the wave is much taller than the volcanic mountain, a perspective that fits. With a faint echo of the fishermen, we're swept up onto the waves, knowing that at any moment the waves are going to crash. Hokusai created a sister print, minus the fishing boats, in which the grasping waves have been replaced with foam tips breaking into a flock of birds— an altogether cheerier view. But his tsunami-like wave and red mountain are the icons that most foreigners identify with all of Japanese art.

Legend has it that Monet happened on Hokusai's work during a trip to Amsterdam, in a food shop where cheap paper decorated with Japanese prints was being used to wrap purchases. The engravings caught his eye. That chance encounter with flimsy, disposable sheets of Oriental wrapping paper would change Western art forever and color how we see the world. Monet fell under the spell of Hokusai and began collecting woodblock prints, in time possessing over two hundred and fifty. It was Hokusai's suite of landscapes, *Thirty-six Views of Mount Fuji*, in which the sacred mountain, always on the rim of Tokyo's awareness, constantly changes while remaining recognizable, that most likely inspired Monet to create his own chromatic series of *Mornings on the Seine*, *Rouen Cathedral*, and *Water Lilies*.

Hokusai belonged to the Edo period in Japan (1615–1868), two centuries of political and social stability, when a fashion of art known as Ukiyo-e ("the floating world") swept the country. Originally a somber Buddhist word meaning the "transient world," where suffering is certain and only impermanence reigns, it was retranslated in 1616 in an altogether less gloomy mood to include "the pleasures of the moon, the snow, the cherry blossoms and the maple-leaves, singing songs, drinking wine . . . and floating. . . ." Its premise: If everything comes to pass, then why not float from one vest-pocket happiness to the next? Its produce: a democratic celebration of the everyday, with zeal and humor, and a passion for visual trivia that's not at all trivial, but what flickers across consciousness from moment to moment, the raw sensations of being alive. Some of the Edo artists' work is quirky, obscene, almost caricature: politicos, fisherwomen, courtesans, actors, street life, family dramas. But other work details the fleeting impressions of weather and landscape, something Monet embraced as a confirmation that his vision was timeless and shared by everyone everywhere, whether or not they could express it.

So Monet's roots reach into Japanese Buddhism, which inspired the floating world movement, which included Hokusai, who inspired Monet to see and paint the fugitive beauty of each moment, which inspires me to limn a skein of dawns. But whereas Hokusai depicted Mount Fuji from dozens of assorted and evocative viewpoints (near to far, emblem to idol), Monet favored one angle on his subjects, which never occupy the background. In Monet's series paintings everything is foreground, as he traces their fleeting impressions in restless light and weather.

Instead of the traditional scenes of historic epics and tales, aristocrats, or stylized birds and flowers, shoguns, samurais, and geishas, Hokusai drew the rhythms of everyday life for the common man and woman, and brought a touching empathy to the drawings. He introduced the direct observation of nature, in many atmospheric conditions, with a special love for water in motion. Working in all the media of his day, from silkscreen to erotic "pillow" drawings, he also invented the *Manga* (a series of sketchbooks, in which he depicts the minutiae of daily life), and left unfinished a series of illustrations with poems, *One Hundred Poems Explained by the Nurse*, in which he updates and sometimes parodies classic Japanese poems.

I know little of Hokusai's death, or even of his health, except that he had a minor stroke in 1826, which he is said to have "recovered" from, and died twenty-three years later at the age of eighty-nine. That probably happened at dawn, since most heart attacks and strokes do occur at dawn. With supreme modesty, or insecurity, and maybe a little in jest, he exclaimed on his deathbed: "If I had another ten years . . . five years, even, I could have become a *real* painter."

ON THE LEDGE OF
THE MORNING

~

Watching the lotuses floating in the pond
was my only relief from the heat.

—SEI SHŌNAGON, *THE PILLOW BOOK*

UNDER A CARTOUCHE OF CLOUDS, I turn off Route 13
and drive toward the lakeshore, where the first sight that
greets me is a small lotus pond. There, like an array of radio
telescopes searching for extraterrestrial life, fifty giant round
leaves lift their faces to the sky. Towering up between them are
twenty or so stage microphones. That can't be right. No, they're
dry pods on tall stems, each perforated with large teardrop-
shaped holes: perfectly designed seed shakers. Dry, they make
brittle brown rattles that go *shak-shak-shak* when shaken. The
flowers procreate only in death, rattling seeds into the pond
if smacked hard (or their necks break). Like daisies, lotuses
bloom at dawn. In the soft morning light, three blossoms open
luminous pink bowls with white flanks that drain to sungold
at the base. Each one is large enough to cup a human face in
its fragrant basin of petals.

The water crumples in sunlight, and green leaf pads are
floating silk. Looking just like water lilies, they're technically a

cousin that thrives in the Middle East. In the Egyptian temple at Edfu, about sixty miles upriver from Luxor, one can find many scenes of a pharaoh offering lotus to the sun god Horus. And in the Turin Papyrus—early pornographic literature—men and women wear a single lotus atop the head, lotus garlands around the neck, and lotus flowers decorating long plaited hair. Lotus was clearly revered, but what did it do or symbolize? Was it an aphrodisiac, a hallucinogen, a narcotic? Hieroglyphics often show pharaohs and consorts sniffing the flower or adding it to wine. The Egyptian lotus's chemical profile includes some unusual bioflavinoids (which influence the color of plants, but act like drugs in humans). It contains a heavy dose of chemicals similar to those in ginkgo biloba, and so it may well have eased memory loss, blood flow problems in general, and impotence. It would have served royally as a health aid and sexual enhancer, a floral Viagra.

Monet would have loved this lily pond and glacial lake haunted by fog ghosts, and the dragon boaters—the "Gorges Dragons"—who ply the water in long dragon-headed barques paddled by teams of twenty, and the bohemian flavor of the early-morning market. In Monet's Floating World that was literally afloat—his boat fitted out with grooves to hold a dozen or so canvases—he loved to watch the ever-changing reflections on the water, and even had his gardeners dust the surface of the water so that the reflections stayed clean. In a sense both practical and mystical, he said he sought "the envelope, the same light spreading everywhere," and that the subject was of little importance to him, because he wanted "to paint the air in which are situated the bridge, the home, the boat."

Unlike Hokusai, who renamed himself repeatedly, Monet kept only one name throughout his life, though in later years he described himself as a painter-gardener "simply mad about flowers." His seven children addressed him formally as "Monet," as did his second wife, Alice. I find that a little odd, but maybe he existed for them as a slightly mythic toiler in paint and light, more so even than as papa or sweetheart.

As Monet grew older and progressively less mobile, he changed the subjects of his paintings from haystacks, fields, and cities to the poplar-lined Seine near home, where he could slowly drift or moor his floating studio beside a bank. When even those forays took their toll and his physical range narrowed, but not his mental scope, he began painting the garden beside his house. If anything it took more imagination to paint without the *rah-rah* of cities and perpetual geisha of a changing scene. Instead, as he aged, he explored the recesses of the familiar: the teal-green Japanese bridge weathering in sun, the water garden and sky conjoining in rain, the buttery noon sun spread across the grass, the rocking goblet-sized tulips and dangling purple wisteria in spring, summer's garden pathway tolling with orange and yellow nasturtiums. Life's constant flickering, rocking, dangling, tolling. The new automatically attracts the eye, but remove the siren of novelty and one must pay attention on purpose, even to subtle tones and totterings, as unrest streaks through the landscape.

Maybe it makes sense, then, that he spent the last twenty years of his life collecting all the known varieties of water lilies, and painting only them. Called *nymphéas* in French, they conjure up a tribe of nubile nymphs swimming naked in the water. In the Buddhist world of Monet's predecessor Hokusai, the water lily symbolized enlightenment because, although its roots flourish in the opaque mud, its flower reaches into the air and fills with nothing but sky. When art critic Maurice Guillemot visited Monet in August 1917, he wrote: "On the glassy surface of the water float *nymphéas*, those extraordinary aquatic plants whose large leaves spread wide and whose exotic blossoms are curiously unsettling." Unsettling? How could they be otherwise seen through Monet's eyes. He immersed himself in their spell, day after day, always seeing them in a new light, with his full regard, as if stumbling upon them for the first time.

DEW DROP IN

~

The breeze at dawn has secrets to tell you.
Don't go back to sleep.

—RUMI (THIRTEENTH CENTURY)

AFTER AN HOUR OF HEAVY rain in tunnel-blackness, first light reveals a fog cloud hugging the grass. How long has it been right in front of me, invisibly close and an acre wide? A giant *fogbow* appears in the rising light. This one shines blue to orange and arches across the road like a mystical staircase. I've known them be double the size of common rainbows and sweep 360 degrees to include the whole vista. One morning, in soupy fog at Point Reyes National Seashore, I lay down in the path of a fogbow, which looked like it was flowing straight through me, then *abracadabra* the light trick vanished.

As the fog rolls away, sunrise is heralded first by ribbons of color—pink, yellow, and blue stripes rising over the edge of the earth and floating up in parallel toward a quickly bluing sky. It's not really blue, it's everything but blue—as fat lumbering blue rays skid off tiny dust particles and ricochet across the sky, we see a *sky blue* day above us. The clearest air is dusty from soil, volcanic debris, and pollution, and of course human skin flecks.

The rising sun paints them with color. So much lies beneath and beyond any sight, including this most familiar one: the blue sky hides the black vacuum of space that carries us briefly from nothing and nowhere, and then back again.

I walk slowly around the garden, which always looks freshest after a rain or when lustrous with dew. In Japan, hosts sometimes mist their garden so that guests arriving for tea will find dewdrops and mistbows.

A tiny snail sits high atop a daylily leaf. Its shell the color of violin resin, it glides to the edge, eye-tipped tentacles waving, and leans over, hunting for the next toehold. I like the hard and soft of a snail, how it smooths its way through the world, its eponymous slowness and feats of high-wire bravado. I like its anything-goes, do-it-yourself hermaphroditic sex life. I like the snail's tongue, an escalator lined with tiny shovels that cut and scrape vegetation. When the shovel-teeth wear down, new ones march forward much as shark teeth do. And, of course, I like its love darts.

Snails court by first stabbing each other with darts carried in a foot quiver. Made of calcium carbonate (think limestone), the darts are sharp as arrowheads. They're also costly, since they use up the calcium a snail needs to craft its shell and coat its eggs. So if a wooer is loaded with love darts, he/she must be nimble and healthy with calcium to spare. Rarely is a suitor's bank account so prickly.

Don't seductive snails ever lie about their wealth? Nope. Snails may be sloppy but they're honest. Most creatures truthfully advertise good health. Hence the jazz of energetic birds singing *Pick ME, pick ME, pick ME!* We're the animals that create elaborate cons on the lathe of our cunning.

I also like how snails crawl, and that one needn't be small

to crawl. Not even lazy or slow. Walruses crawl when they're on land. Through tough muscle power, earthworms crawl by erecting stiff bristles that grab a surface, then push off. Snakes use their delving scales to crawl fast (anger a black mamba and it can chase you at 6 miles per hour while holding its head up). Humans crawl on land and through water. Masters of fancy footwork, and always at home and under roof, a snail is a seashell by any other name. Not a toe-tapper. More of a one-footed skier, a slime-o-pod. As electrical waves spur its muscular foot, first one section sticks to the ground, then the next, and so flesh glides.

Just when this snail seems doomed to topple, it issues mucous from a gland and slides along its own unravelings to a lower leaf. At last it ankles off into the undergrowth, hunting a suitable target for its love darts, and leaving behind only a sticky trail to collect dew.

Busy spiders have been toiling through the night, and their well-engineered webs are sparkling insect-traps, weighted by dew. Some spin a loose maze of silk, others carefully embroider doilies and funnels. A black and yellow argiope spider is hanging head down on the outside of my window. She seems to be floating in midair. It's only when I get very close, tilt my head, and look askance that her delicate web of zigzag bands pops into view, she herself poised in its exact center, doing theater in the round. A virtuoso of touch, she has spun a web so nearly invisible that it's bound to catch wayward insects. One shudder of the web and she'll pounce. She is an "orb-weaver," she engineers worlds. Slipping across her web like a hand on an autoharp, she lives music, sensing her prey by vibration. At first, she doesn't glimpse the prey itself, only the havoc it displays, only its panic.

My big eyes and head don't seem to bother her. Nor does the drafty hummingbird only a foot above her at a feeder. Argiopes have poor eyesight, despite their eight eyes. Only the front two eyes discriminate, the others add peripheral clues. When something quivers her web, she just focuses on the number of legs—six means food, eight means a possible mate. She could be a character in George Orwell's allegorical novella *Animal Farm*, where the totalitarian animal leaders decree: "four legs good, two legs bad." Our prejudices are sometimes as concise as a spider's.

Scientists are always messing around with orb-weavers, giving them drugs (doused on a fly) that cause them to change the pattern of their web, or turning the web in a frame to test how gravity influences them. Sometimes researchers pull aside a few strands while the spider is spinning to see if she'll revise her blueprints and compensate (she does). In the summer of 1973, two spiders named *Anita* and *Arabella* became the first spidernauts, going into orbit aboard *Skylab III*. The webs they wove in picture frames matched ones spun on earth, but the texture of the silk differed—thinner overall and uneven, with thicker and thinner patches, as the spiders tried to control the silk's elasticity in weightlessness.

Back on Earth, NASA later tested psychotropic drugs on spiders, and learned: LSD inspires a web in the shape of a sunburst with wide rays shooting out from a center disk. On benzedrine, a spider spins a fast jazzy web, riddled with large holes. After taking chloral hydrate (sleeping pills), a spider drapes a few threads together in a loose hammock. Caffeine has a chaotic effect—threads reeled together at jagged angles, creating a web a Cubist like Picasso might have drawn. The more toxic the drug the more deformed the web.

Wherever webs happen, in whatever delirium, they all begin by free-falling, then pulling silk from the belly to weld small bridges across the emptiness. An orb-weaver at my back door has tapped her belly and spun a line between the hummingbird feeder and the screen door handle. From there it's plain geometry. When all is done, she sits at the hub of the web, head down, eight legs outstretched, waiting for the next morsel to get stuck. The hovering hummingbirds sometimes flutter her silk, and I imagine she has false alarms, when her senses tell her she has caught a meal, only to be disappointed. With an exquisitely tuned sense of touch, she feels the telltale struggle of a moth, a fly, a cricket, as it sends unique shivers up her legs. And as each hair vibrates in a slightly different direction, she pinpoints the exact whereabouts of her prey. Does she have preferences—crunchy, caustic, fat, gooey—and race to one meal, meander to another? I think so. Spiders carefully cut around some insects and let them drop from their webs. And the hunting spider *Portia* only needs to encounter a spitting spider once to develop a taste for it, keep it in mind, and search for it while ignoring flies and other prey. Ignoble as we may find them, even spiders can be picky, form mental images, and make choices. We dismiss them as small-minded, senseless, disposable, yet each is a being solid and fragile as glass, an expanse of life. How odd that we wonder about the lives of alien civilizations when we know so little about the aliens among us, the other animals with whom we share our lives, but whose experiences, even the most elemental, elude us.

As the sun rises behind her web, it illuminates her in the center of a small coliseum. She is a young female, spotted black and yellow, less than an inch long, and her web is heavily zigzagged with more crisscrosses than she really needs or adults require. But so it goes with the young and their gobs of energy. As they mature they learn to spin better webs with fewer strands, how to use their energy more efficiently, what is overkill, and the minimum it takes to dive into thin air and spin bridges that flow into one another. She sits in the eye of a stationary tornado, waiting. Like all weaving, the gossamer sags here and there, is taut and tightly knit elsewhere. In this light it looks like it's made of silvery-gray wire, not threads of silk whose evenly spaced diamonds are drops of silk glue. Spinning several kinds of silk, she knows not to walk on the sticky parts, or she'd be trapped in her own lair!

Meanwhile, in the garage, a funnel spider has constructed a beautiful large web that falls and swells like a computer graph of celestial mechanics. At the far end of her tablecloth she sits in a cave of silk, legs arched and ready. Her cloth is decorated with the carcasses of flies, mosquitoes, and other unidentifiable small creatures hapless enough to flit in. She waits to pounce. A transparent mountain slope, the web hangs off the window screen at one extreme, hooks onto the draping window frame, then cascades two feet and laces up with an old cycling bag. Stern to stern it's three feet across, but there is no warp to its weft. Clearly it was laid down in long sticky banners, one next to the other, with overlapping strings haphazardly intersecting.

As engineering, it swoops like a suspension bridge in the Alps. From below, it appears to be a lace ceiling beyond which the windowed world appears, veil beyond veil. From above, it's barely visible, and since it changes topography so much, a fleeing insect would hit a sticky rope at many different angles. All the corpses lie on top of the web, not dangling beneath. The underside is smoother and more predictable, without the ghostly towers and tepees. It could look even stranger: I've read about a South American spider that chops up its corpses and reassembles them in her own image to confuse predators into thinking she has allies!

Does she see me? Is she watching back? When I blow across her web, making it tremble, she doesn't budge. Even when I touch the web lightly with a twig or drop a leaf fleck onto it, she sits still. I would need to toss her a live wriggling bug, and I haven't the heart.

Elsewhere, garden slugs that shimmied up the tallest day-lilies, then slid down slime ropes unraveled from their loins, have left pretty streamers glittering with dew behind them. No dew forms on me, or on most other animals for that matter, since we're warmer than vegetation, not shiny or smooth, rarely cooler than air.

Because our brains love the up and down of things, we say that night and dew fall, but night is a mammoth shadow that slowly gathers around one's ankles, and dew whispers through a garden when water condenses near the ground on cool nights. Morning dew is but a small part of that old drama in which cougar and cloud are cousins, and water is a treasure always borrowed, never lost. Perfect little prisms, dew will flash spectral colors one by one—blue, green, yellow, orange—if you condense your thoughts for a moment and move snail-slow past a single drop.

Over a thousand years ago, a young Sei Shōnagon came in from the dawn and told her *Pillow Book* of the glorious dew, because there was no one else who would understand: "Despite the bright sun, dew was still dripping from the chrysanthemums in the garden. On the bamboo fences and criss-cross hedges I saw tatters of spider webs; and where the threads were broken the raindrops hung on them like strings of white pearls. I was greatly moved and delighted. As it became sunnier, the dew gradually vanished from the clover and the other plants where it had lain so heavily; the branches began to stir, then suddenly sprang up of their own accord. Later I described to people how beautiful it all was. What most impressed me was that they were not at all impressed."

WHERE IT'S SUMMER

~

Oh, to seep out of bed on a summer morning, trailing dream rag-ends after you, to find a bright full-size dream still in play. In many ways this is the finest time of the year: The roses bellow scent and cascade over obelisks and each other. Squirrel babies are feeding and mischiefing all over the yard and roof, skittering across the skylights, robbing the bird feeders. At any moment, a quick flick of a newt will flit up a garden fence and start doing push-ups to attract a mate. Groundhogs come right onto the back patio, hummingbirds are braver around humans, and skunks and raccoons peer through the screen doors. Tiny haunting eyes shine red at night. Tall trees have leafed out into a vast wall of privacy. Yellow sundrops ignite all the flower beds. Orange daylilies trumpet from the roadsides. And the voice-dueling birds keep winding their springs, buzzing their kazoos, whistling, warbling, and chattering in a divine ruckus of warring songs.

Summer lives in the shadows of old trees striping the road,

the hurry-up-and-wait jumping of squirrels, and the pungent magenta ruffles of roses rocking gently like pomanders, their perfume so bakery-sweet I can't resist smelling them over and over until my sated nose gives up, exhausted. The only news this morning is that a yellow-throated lily has appeared near the bay window, and the ligularia has raised a dozen flat radardish leaves even higher and tauter in the dappled shade.

The rising sun bleaches everything it touches—now the lawn, the gray fence, the cream slats of a neighbor's house, the bald hedges two barely antlered young bucks stripped down to the bark yesterday. *How you've grown,* I found myself saying silently, remembering them with buttons on their foreheads only a month or so ago. Do they have growing pains, as humans do in adolescence? It occurs to me that I don't know the sound of a deer in pain.

Parent catbirds, goldfinches, robins, jays, wrens, blackbirds, and sparrows are all running a proper shuttle service, providing hundreds of mouthfuls for their chicks. When their paths cross at the nest, they usually do a fluff-and-quiver dance on nearby branches to plight their troth. If they arrive with a small green tidbit, the babies squawk in unison.

In the apple tree, a female catbird stays inside its nest with the chicks while the male delivers food. I don't know if she eats what he gives her to keep her strength up while tending the brood, or if she's there to macerate the food first and then feed it to the young. It's always easier if a parent pre-digests food a little for its offspring. We do the same thing by cutting up and cooking food, I suppose, and it amuses me that mouth-feeding is the most likely origin of French kissing. In the not-so-distant past (and in the present among some "traditional" people, as doctors discovered in a couple of unusual cases of

HIV transmission), human mothers pre-chewed food for their infants, just as birds and other animals do, and passed the food by mouth and tongue into their baby's mouth. When the infants grew up, they retained loving associations with deep kissing, and that trick worked so well in pair-bonding that the kissing remains, even when the pre-digesting doesn't. In chic restaurants today, one can order "macerated" greens, and whenever I see the word I'm reminded of bird mash, French kissing, and how we've never gotten over our yen for mom's semi-digested food.

A humid, overcast sky; the air feels like cloud. On soggy mornings dragonflies and birds fly low over the earth hunting insects close to the ground. The air sags heavy with water droplets, suspended, refusing to rain. I may see and describe it as *still*, yet each second contains a legion of events. Even the so-called still air is twitching and aglow, churned by currents imperceptible to me but carrying spores and birds, insects and leaves, fungi and pollen, viruses and gases. And it is never still for long, but always everywhere fidgetingly alive. A stillness of winds strong enough to bend trees and move oceans of sand, erode hillsides, sculpt shorelines, sow seeds far and wide. The still world is too quick to behold, the silent world clamors with noise.

I wish I could hear the ultrasonic squeaks of mice, who seem to have almost as many calls as we do, from a pup's squealing *I'm lost! Where are you, Mom?!* to a male's ultrasonic grunting thrusts during sex. I try to picture all the crickets listening through eardrum-like membranes on their knees, all the cicadas listening likewise through their bellies. Because I can't *hear* the mice, it helps if I *picture* them, even though I can't really see them. And even if I did see them, I wouldn't just be seeing them but also remembering them. Brain-mapping shows that two-thirds of vision is *memory*, not what's happening in the occipital lobes! When I see a magnolia branch, my brain provides an image of the full tree, when I hear a rat-a-tat-tat, my brain riffles through its images for a woodpecker viewed one morning last fall. Memories are always true to the moment of recall. Each time we haul them up from the brain's sloshy attic, we primp and prune them in terms of the here and now, and store them as slightly different mementos. As we grow and change, each memory adapts so that we feel real and fuel a continuous sense of self. And so every generation experiences a unique version of history, and everyone revises memories over time.

July will be a scorcher for those of us on life's Serengeti, by which I mean all of us. But it's also a time pitted with reminders of how many days have fled. Now I'm stung by the same elements that surprise and delight me: the bees' golden pantaloons as they collect nectar with increased urgency, the beautiful hedges of ornamental grasses that began the summer flush with the ground and now offer a gauntlet of five-foot-high spears, the longer time the hummers spend at the feeder, fattening up as fast as possible for migration—only two months away. Of course, summer does not exist in the mossy-brown bark of the magnolia, chocolate in the blur of rain. Not even in the indigo's fat seedpods, each one a plump lady's leg with a seamed stocking. Summer exists only in the mind of the beholder. Peering through the spectacles of tree limbs and watching the nectar-gathering of bees, we bring summer to this so-called July, whose days wear numbers only if counted.

WOODPECKER DAWN

～

I LIVE NEAR SAPSUCKER WOODS, named after the yellow-
bellied sapsucker, a beautiful woodpecker with black and
white feathers, red cap and throat, and a pale yellow belly. As
its name celebrates, it adores the sweet syrup hidden below a
tree's bark. Each year, sapsuckers fly north when the sap starts
running in the spring, and tap necklaces of small holes around
tree limbs. Sap trickles down in dark ribbons. I've seen a bird
visit its wells repeatedly, licking sap with a brushy tongue. In
time, the tree sap scabs over the holes, and then the woodpecker taps another ring of wells above or below the first. A
hungry sapsucker has left four necklaces around a central limb
of my magnolia. I don't know what magnolia sap tastes like;
and insects drawn to any sap get trapped in sticky amber and
add tasty slivers of protein to the nectar-like drink. Local sapsuckers seem to prefer the softer bark of aspens and magnolias,
and bore holes in several branches at a time, in the process filling the air with drumrolls. They telegraph their whereabouts as
they set to work drilling and mining, while also guarding their

wells. Many species of birds wait for the jackhammer-jawed sapsuckers to do what they can't—drill down to the fount of sweet flowing sap—and steal in to lap up sap and insects when the owner is working another claim site.

During the summer, sapsuckers wound the trees by tattooing one string of pearls after another. Sap is blood-precious to a tree, which thickens to seal up the wounds, but sapsucker saliva may work as an anticoagulant, allowing the tonic to pour.

This isn't the pungent sap that maple syrupers tap in early spring, a watery fluid that flows up to the leaves at such a pace it's easy for humans to cup. According to the Iroquois, a New York State tribe, long ago a boy watched squirrels lapping maple sap in winter and tasted it himself, delighted by the sweetness. From then on, maple syrup became a human staple. But maple is a harder wood for sapsuckers to pierce. Magnolia sap offers a rich enough prize. It's small wonder hummingbirds arrive right on the heels of sapsuckers in the spring, before many flowers ooze with nectar, having flown from Mexico, Central America, and the West Indies—lands of sun, spice, and blossom—to the comparative chill of our summer, to breed and brood without breaking a sweat.

In my yard, the hummingbirds are partial to magnolia sap and have learned how to rob it from the sapsuckers. Phoebes, warblers, and other birds rush to the open wells, too, but the spear-toting hummingbirds attack all but the sapsuckers, their benefactors. And the sapsuckers employ the hummers as armed angels who keep the sap-guzzling heavies at bay. Humans have felt the same about water holes, the source of many a feud. If this is racketeering, it's a widespread, ancient tit-for-tat that works. Nature doesn't care if one's annoyed, or how cumbersome the process may be, only that, ultimately, it wins.

Nearby, sitting on her well-camouflaged, lichen-lined nest, a sheen-green hummingbird waits patiently for the sapsucker to leave, then darts in for a snootful from the sarsaparilla bar. Only two hummers this year, and I'm trying to experience my disappointment not as anger or depression or *I want*, but just as one more feeling among the day's phenomena: the sunlight shining separate lamps through the leaves of the magnolia, the buds atop a slender daylily stem, the house moaning when someone turns on the faucet in the woods, the glassy clatter of dishes being washed in the kitchen, writing in a journal whose cover is a reproduction of Hokusai's famous wave, the rictus of pain in my neck, the steep plunge of my eyes down to paper, disappointment, the glowing patch covering a small hole in the window screen, how everything vanishes when eyelids fall, as though the whole plush buzzing world wasn't, couldn't be, hasn't been.

The noise yanks my lids up again. Woodpecker dawns always begin with a loud syncopated drumming, reverberating around the neighborhood. Unlike a bird, I can't pinpoint the direction of these drumbeats, some log-low, some rat-a-tat, all echoing like mad from the trees.

How odd that a group of woodpeckers is called a *descent*, unless one considers the lofty perch they once occupied in Greek myth. The witch Circe, who excelled at concocting magical potions and herbs, really didn't like being rebuffed. As the daughter of the Sun, she rose each day with a boiling temper and had a bad habit of changing into an animal anyone who piqued her. One morning, she was gathering herbs when she spotted the handsome demigod Picus, a trickster she desired who didn't give her the time of day. In a stellar fury, Circe scalded him with her wand, morphing him into a woodpecker.

The myth doesn't specify what sort of woodpecker Picus became, but all woodpeckers are tools—tip to toe woodworking tools—with muscled neck, chisel bill, long sticky tongue of barbed hairs, thick skull, and a brain cushioned by a layer of air. Even the nostrils are a bristled mask to filter out wood chips and debris. The only reason woodpeckers don't bash their brains out or concuss or pass out is because their brain sits above their beak on sturdy shock absorbers. But Picus was doomed to hammer trees at 25 miles per hour, banging his head all day long.

What stripe of woodpecker? Given Circe's lust and spite, Picus may have been a pileated, the huge redhead that creates a racket excavating trees at dawn. One living in my yard has gouged big rectangles into both sides of a tall dead oak, carving its own private feeding trough. I wish it all the carpenter ants it can find. Its crackerjack blows carry down the street, and it nests in the tallest trees, despite the lightning hazard.

Or Picus may have become a red-bellied woodpecker, an altogether smaller gent with a striking black and white zebra pattern on his back, a blaze of red from forehead to nape of the neck, and just a smudge of red on the belly feathers.

Half past sunrise one morning, when the doorbell rang twice, I went to answer it and, finding no one there, sauntered back to my study. Again the bell rang, more urgently this time, but again there was no one standing out front. It rang again, insistently. Hiding, I watched, and to my astonishment a red-bellied woodpecker perched beside the door and used the bell as a "signal post," bashing the metal button over and over to attract a mate, obviously besotted with the sound.

GLORY DAYS

~

Even if I ride the wings of the dawn, and dwell in the
uttermost parts of the sea . . .

—PSALM 139:9

A LONG BLUE TUBE SURGES across the Adirondack sky:
what looks like a giant shock wave stretching from horizon to horizon, rushing forward while spinning backward, in
the process sucking up moist air with furious abandon, while
swirling all the dust and leaves below. Could it really be a cloud
glory? Long rolling clouds, complete with wind squalls, wind
shear, and fast updrafts, glories sometimes launch severe thun-
derstorms. The visible cloud glories, I mean. Invisible cloud
glories haunt the earth's skies in all seasons, at all altitudes,
and some people think they may be the ghostly cause of wind
shear. In Ithaca, we certainly have our share of wind shear,
and also a gulf-like lake to collect glory. Still, it's the first cloud
glory I've ever seen here, a long gut of gusty air riding on a cold
front. Passing overhead, the cloud rolls darkness into light,
as if painting the dawn. Then the air hangs flat. A glory can
stop the wind.

That wouldn't surprise the Aborigines of northern Australia, who call cloud glories *yibibis*, and summon them with a stomping dance, because glories herald the wet hunting season, when fish run, new grass grows, and the bush nuts and figs ripen in heavy dew. For them, it's a gala time of abundance, the opposite of risk, a far cry from the sport of glory-surfing that unfolds above them.

On autumn mornings, when cloud glories smear Australia's Gulf of Carpentaria, glider pilots pilgrimage to the outback hamlet of Burketown (population 235) to surf the leading edge of some wave clouds as long as Britain. Burketown is small enough to picture in one thought: a nearly inaccessible settlement that consists of a school, a pub, a service station, and three general stores gracing a bleak Martian landscape of snake-riddled savannas and salt pans. For glider pilots, the glories create dangerous wind squalls, and the gulf isn't a good place to ditch since it's infested with crocodiles. But this unusual dawn sport has been drawing gliders and hang gliders alike for over twenty years. As if surfing a rogue ocean wave, pilots perform maneuvers in the powerful spill at the wave front, and let the huge push fling them far inland.

Only about 20 aircraft surf the glory each year, steered by pilots who are thrill-seekers, joyriders, oddity collectors, or cloud enthusiasts—among them a Qantas pilot from Mooloo-laba near Brisbane; a charter member of the Cloud Appreciation Society from England; the owner of the town's only light aircraft charter service; and a professor of earth sciences from Canberra. They will be there right now, checking their rigging and eagerly watching the skies. Predicting a cloud glory has become a local art akin to dousing, because glories need a sweet spot of humidity and only form at dawn. Pilots know the signs of approaching glory: an unusually heavy dew, with the wooden tabletops in the Savanna Lodge's café bending at the corners, the pub's fridge doors frosting over, the beer cooler sweating, and a thin dark line edging the horizon. Ken, a fifty-something microlight pilot from Melbourne, will have driven twelve days through the outback, as he does each year, for a ride that's unparalleled, the ultimate gliding adventure: "Despite the forces that are at work as this wave is rolling along, the air that you are gliding through is as clear as crystal. When you are on the morning glory, you are surfing a cloud."

Long before cloud-glory pilots, William Wordsworth wrote in his *Ode: Intimations of Immortality from Recollections of Early Childhood*:

> *Our birth is but a sleep and a forgetting:*
> *The Soul that rises with us, our life's Star,*
> *Hath had elsewhere its setting,*
> *And cometh from afar:*
> *Not in entire forgetfulness,*
> *And not in utter nakedness,*
> *But trailing clouds of glory do we come.*

Surfing clouds of glory—literally or in an ecstasy of imagining—we return to the freshness of childhood and a rapport with nature that bubbles up so naturally, Wordsworth says, that it's "a thought too deep for tears."

Glories arise as part of the continent's natural breathing, with cool sea air flowing onto the hot land during the day, and warm land air breathing out at night. Colliding breaths build a turbulent mountain of air that, when it collapses, throws a shock wave ahead of the spreading spill. Not a phenomenon limited to our planet—scientists have sighted possible cloud glories in the atmosphere of Mars, and pioneers may one day surf them. Like so much of nature, glories exist though we can't see them, unless the conditions are just right and we're open to possibility.

Dawn is also the hour of hot-air balloonists and soloing student pilots, who prefer a frappé of still air; and it's the time for "dawn patrolling"—what Hawaiian surfers call early-morning wave riding. As surfer Joelle Tafoya enthuses: "It's an indescribable feeling when you drop down the face, pull into a stand-up barrel, and see the sunrise over Diamond Head." Less wind at dawn makes it safer, but sharks also feed most at dawn when their prey becomes visible.

In Ithaca, dawn is the hour of a lemming-like plunge of nearly three hundred women into Lake Cayuga for "Women Swimmin'." This fund-raiser for the local hospice takes place every August, when the lake is at its warmest (high 70s), and begins at dawn when the water is calmer and there's little boat traffic. Our long, deep glacial lake narrows at its southern tip, the 1.2-mile crossing takes about forty-five minutes, and every swimmer garners sponsors (last year's swim raised over a hundred thousand dollars). Women join the swim for many reasons, but often as a tribute to a relative or friend who died of breast cancer. Hospicare is much beloved here, where many families have been touched by its end-of-life care. Although a bad knee keeps me from swimming the lake myself, I sponsor a friend and her daughter, in memory of my mother.

The dawn swimmers, standing on the shore, looking back over their lives—what do they see? Striving? Years lost to ambition? Worry bogs? The joy of loving and being loved? A sunlit, baggy adventure full of steep emotions? Like the Kumbh Mela celebrants, they are drawn down to misty water on the threshold of the day for a raucous commingling of life and death. Entering the lake's stony darkness, they swim the morning into being and emerge onto the far shore for breakfast, exhausted but also exhilarated. Their fatigue reminds me of a wonderful passage in David Whyte's *Midlife and the Great Unknown*, in which he tells of a visit from a monk friend, to whom David confides feeling bone-weary, waterlogged, and windless. His friend listens with concern in the dwindling hours of the night, and then says something that still gives me pause: "You know, the antidote to exhaustion is not rest. It's wholeheartedness."

AUTUMN

THE MURMURING OF
INNUMERABLE BEES

W HEN THE DARK DYE OF night washes away and the
stars melt back into space, a cloud locomotive chugs
behind the ridges. The sky blues until even Venus fades, the
light quickens, then a six-pointed sun sparkles among the
leaves. Turning in its sleep, the whole planet begins to wake
and slowly go about its life.

The purple aster saloons are closed, their cupped doors
pursed shut, and no bee may enter before opening time. But
that's okay, since it's 8:01 on a Sunday morning and the bees
aren't up yet. At 41 degrees it's too chilly to fly. Some of the
honeybees will be huddled in their hives, balled up and warm.
Others, like the three I see snoozing among trefoil blossoms,
look dead, but actually slowed to a stall as the night cool sank.
On cold nights, they need the group hug of hive mates to keep
warm. Unlike honeybees (and humans for that matter), bumblebees don't store food and huddle indoors, staying sociable
and warm during winter. Instead most of their family dies,

leaving behind only young pregnant females who hibernate belowground, hanging fat and silent, waiting in suspense for spring. Bees are precise timekeepers, who know dandelions and water lilies open at 7:00 a.m., marigolds at 9:00 a.m., and evening primroses not until 6:00 p.m. But this time of year foragers often can't make it back to the hive before dark, or are ragged or beaten up, and so they settle en route to wait out the night. Most die in the process. They look glued in place, as many animals do early on spring and fall mornings. With the rising sun and heat of the day, the asters will yawn wide and the surviving bees begin to stir.

8:15 a.m. The bees are still asleep, wax-museum style, the asters still closed for business. But the sun has coated the top branches of the magnolia tree with honeyed light. Lower down, gnats occasionally flicker across the windowpane and one large lumbering primate alternately writes in a purple-covered note-book and eats from a bowl of oatmeal and blueberries, sips from a cup of dark strong alkaloid flavored with the ductal secretions of a pregnant cow.

At last, one stem of asters begins to sway ever so slightly, as two purple flowers open enough to reveal gold majorette tassels inside their cave. An early jogger trots down the street with a yellow dog on a short leash by his side. The primate has covered his body with a thick coat and his head with a cap. I imagine the dog is chilly, too, despite the fluttering ribbons of lemon light as the sun climbs the sky.

The way I bespoke the physics of sun and earth is all wrong, of course, since, as I noted earlier, the sun doesn't really climb the sky. But there are only so many truths one wants to keep in mind at a time. We humans are adept at knowing and not knowing, while knowing somewhere at the edge of the moment that that's what we're doing. Still, it's soothing to follow the soft enchantment of sun as it spotlights a few brown planks on a neighbor's house or washes one small area of mown lawn with stagelights, leaving the rest in shadow.

Sometime during the night, the pink and yellow petals of a rose cascaded to the ground, where they now lie among untidy blades of grass. Most of the aster flowers are still closed, their pollen out of reach behind silky shutters. Mind you, there's lots of nectar and pollen nearby: the showy sedum, looking like rows of pink broccoli; the black-eyed Susans and their smaller cousins, the brown-eyed Susans; fairy roses galore; yellow and paprika-red yarrow; magenta dahlias; pink coneflowers; pollen-colored ligularia; blue lobelias. There's plenty to feed on. And though it's now 8:50 a.m., the wayward honeybees are still asleep.

Atop an indigo leaf, a fat hairy bumblebee slumbers, motionless. The breeze jolts her leaf, but the bee still seems buttoned in place. I can just imagine the fate of the bee, out foraging yesterday and unable to make it back to the hive before dark, having to grab a leaf and wait through night chill for dawn. If I were this bee, an older female (because younger ones stay home to help in the nursery), I'd be waiting for the first breath of sunlight and the morning damp to dry. At last I'd tilt my head and stir. Two feet would jut out and back in a hokey pokey sort of move, then my wings would flex a little without lifting. Ten minutes later, still not flying, I'd climb to the top of the leaf and amble around. Next I'd begin working the bellows of my abdomen, rhythmically, in a bee version of calisthenics, to limber up my flight muscles. Still no flashing wings, but lots of quiver. Bumblebees can twitch their wing muscles fast to create body heat. A neat trick. My two leg baskets would bulge with pollen, a heavy load to haul home, and I might have misjudged the weight or flying time. Weights and balances are hard enough for a pilot with a slide rule to calculate. Imagine them changing repeatedly during flight! Fortunately, I could gauge wind speed by how far back my antennae were bending. Humans do the same with blowing hair and wind socks. This morning, I might even be suffering from a bad case of jet lag. Jet-setter research bees, flown from France to New York, stay on their usual feeding times until they adapt to the new time zone; before then, they're as easily confused as their human traveling companions. Where is the ground hive, anyway? It's bound to be in a burrow dug by some obliging critter, or maybe a grassy nest stolen from a field mouse. As morning sun finds the fothergilla, I'd flurry my wings, levitate, and lumber away at last, buzzing home with rich cargo.

HONEYCOMBING

⌒

DOWN AT THE FARMERS' MARKET, the local beekeepers
have a booth where they're setting up a foot-long observation hive sealed between panes of glass in a wooden frame.
Some of these bees would normally be out foraging; instead
they roam their vertical island, trying to escape. Georg pulls
up in his old VW bus and waves hello; he has brought his collection of antique rye-straw bee skeps and his seven-year-old
son Martin. When Georg was Martin's age, he had an enclosed
observation hive by his bedroom window, with a tube leading
outside so that the bees could come and go. Years later, as a
college student, he helped run bee experiments, and it was his
job to "tag" the bees.

Today, only the queen bee is marked in this hive, and she's
visible at once as the fat bee with a white crown (of paint) on
her head. All the bees begin as workers, but a queen is transformed by royal jelly, which makes her grow about 40 percent
larger and 60 percent heavier. It's the nurse bees' job to feed

her the jelly. Otherwise, she's genetically identical to all the other bees, just bigger, heartier, and full of the magic elixir that makes her fertile enough to lay three million eggs during her reign. That takes time, of course, so though worker bees only live seven to eight weeks, a queen can live five to seven years. Royal jelly is so knotty and rich it hasn't been fully analyzed yet, but does contain B complex, hormones, pantothenic acid, omega 3s, lecithin, collagen, gamma globulin, and nucleic acids, among other tonics.

A jar of multicolored pollen grains sits on the table:

purple—Joe pye weed
brown—windblown grasses
yellow—goldenrod

I unscrew it and pour a few onto my palm, then tip one grain of goldenrod pollen onto my other palm, rolling it gently back and forth to weigh it. It feels quite heavy for a bee to carry. A few would weigh a honeybee down, and so it's no wonder that some of Georg's returning bees, when they're descending at last to the hive door, miscalculate their descent and land in the grass, then pick themselves up and hop the last small distance.

Buckwheat produces honey with a heavy molasses taste. And loosestrife honey looks green, like virgin olive oil. Bees like pollen from bamboo and knapwood, too. There are many sources of honey in my garden alone: aster (which produces clear, mild honey), goldenrod (the honey has a sort of vinyl aftertaste), linden, black locust, clover, basswood, raspberry— to name only a few. I pop the grain of goldenrod pollen onto my tongue where it melts airily like cotton candy. Headache, neck ache, and fatigue set in, but fortunately I'm only mildly addled.

Back home, I put on a bee suit, sometimes called a "Neil Armstrong suit," complete with pith helmet and netting that ties around the waist, and join Georg to inspect his three hives. The netting makes a snug seal around the head and neck. Otherwise the suit includes loose white overalls and long gloves with elastic ends to create another snug seal. Trouser legs are tucked into tall boots. It takes a little getting used to bees sitting on the nearly invisible net only a few inches from my face, but it's also a good opportunity to eye them. At first, clouded round by bees, I'm tempted to back away. Especially when they buzz louder in an irritated whine. That's what the smoker is for, a quaintly old-fashioned-looking device that's essentially a teapot with a bellows attached to the handle. Old cotton rasp smokes nicely inside, and playing the bellows sends smoke out the spout. A few smoke clouds in the hive and the bees scramble deeper indoors and quiet down almost at once. As Georg lifts the panels out to check on the workers, the fatter (male) drones, and how much honey they're producing, I sedate the crowd with more smoke. The smoke doesn't anesthetize them; it makes them think there's a fire nearby and they fill up on honey just in case they have to abandon the hive. The meal occupies and quiets them. Anyway, that's one theory. Another is that the smoke may mask their pheromones, hide their work orders.

Honeybees are surprisingly mild-mannered and don't attack unless provoked—there's just too much at stake. When they do sting, the poison-filled stinger pulls free to stay in the victim and continue pumping venom, but the bee dies. So they prefer not to fall on their swords. Georg and Lucia have four small children who play in a yard where ninety thousand honeybees roam, and the children are rarely stung. Georg, on the other hand, has been stung so many times during his thirty-some years that he's virtually immune.

Nearby, Cornell University specializes in honeybee research, and the agriculture library contains rows of volumes about bees and beekeeping. Among its rare books is L. L. Langstroth's classic beekeeping book, *The Hive and the Honey-Bee* (1853), in manuscript, and, more precious still, his bizarre diary.

Known as the father of American beekeeping, L. L. Langstroth (1810–1895) invented the movable-frame hive, which radically changed American beekeeping, the economy, and our national sweet tooth by making honey suddenly more plentiful. His journal is the holy grail of beekeepers, many of whom make pilgrimages to the Rare Books Room at Cornell just to touch his classic work in its original form.

On the second floor of Mann Library in the Phillips Beekeeping Special Collection, I surrender my purse, ID, and other belongings. A young conservatory specialist with large blue eyes and honey-colored hair leads me into an open glass-sided cubicle where white cotton gloves and foam wedges wait on a desk. There I am allowed to handle the journal, smell it, carefully turn its fragile pages, and read what I can decipher of it. At one point Langstroth tells of holding a chilly queen bee in his hand and warming her with his breath. A memory flashes to mind: a chilly dawn in California, when I held a just-tagged monarch butterfly to my open mouth and warmed it with my breath so that it could fly to safety.

Reading Langstroth's papers, looking at the photograph of him at eighty, I wonder about his mental illness, which became more and more debilitating, and the role bees played in keeping him sane. Langstroth studied for the ministry at Yale, and was pastor of several Congregational churches in Massachusetts, but suffered terribly from ferocious nerves (while trying to preach his first sermon, he became voiceless and couldn't go on). Crippling depression dogged him throughout his career. Leaving the ministry, he became the principal of a young ladies' school in Philadelphia, and when that proved too much he retired to Dayton, Ohio, where he sometimes preached at the Wayne Avenue Presbyterian Church, despite his paralyzing panic attacks. In Dayton, on October 6, 1895, Langstroth died in the pulpit just as he was launching into a sermon on the love of God.

Although his journal contains a lifetime's unique observations of bees and their world, it has never been published because it's mainly indecipherable. Langstroth wrote in an extravagant scrawl full of curving strokes at speed, and his bouts of depression made his penmanship even worse. Nonetheless, it's prized by beekeepers. There's just one skimpy biography of the man, whose story remains largely a mystery, even though Langstroth led a somewhat public life and kept his bee journal for decades.

Many naturalists have scrawled such journals—John Muir, Henry David Thoreau, and James Audubon come to mind. I feel lucky their journals survive, brimming with observations of vanished wildlife and suffused with wonder. We are the only animal driven to leave such a stamp, a silhouette of itself, on the wind. As deeply as we need to sit under the dome of stars as dawn quickens, and feel that there is something greater than ourselves, so do we need to etch our initials on the trunk of time—even illegibly! Keeping a diary of the self and the world it inhabits seems to me a generous form of that urge, a way of honeycombing experience.

AN ANGLE ON ARCHIMEDES

THE CRESCENT MOON HAS FLED into a landscape of cloud gorges, buttes, and mesas, all interflowing, mute and radiant. As night pours away, the roots of a fallen tree catch the sunlight in a tangle of iridescence, and then the grass emerges, apparently strewn with ancient scrolls. Every fall, the bark of the tall sycamore in the front yard begins to peel off. In time, the ground beneath it grows littered with parchment scrolls reminding me of Archimedes' lost journals, in which he recorded the shapes and angles of nature. Written in Greek on papyrus sometime around 287–212 B.C., the original text included some of his most important works: "On Floating Bodies," "On the Measurement of the Circle," "On the Sphere and the Cylinder," "On Spiral Lines," and "On the Equilibrium of Planes." Here he introduces the idea of pi, 3.14159 ad infinitum, the ratio you get when you divide the circumference of a circle by its diameter. It's a number that never rounds off, and yet we use it today in countless equations that measure everything from ocean waves to economics and chart the travels of spacecraft.

After his death, the scrolls disappeared, never to be found again. But someone had copied them onto another set of papyrus. It was only in around A.D. 1000 that a Constantinople scribe copied them once more, this time onto parchment which he fastened together. Two hundred years later, a monk found the old book, didn't recognize its importance, and decided the bound pages would make a handy prayer book. So he washed or scraped off as much of the original ink as he could and wrote prayers over the faded writing. The prayer book survived fire, plunder, and the Crusades, sitting in a monastery until 1906, when a visiting Danish philologist recognized it as a palimpsest. Using a magnifying glass, he identified Archimedes' text below the prayers, deciphered what he could, and published that as a book. However, the palimpsest itself disappeared sometime after 1908 and during the 1930s a forger decorated it in gold leaf on several pages to boost its value, despite the greater treasure lying beneath the medieval prayers.

A French collector bought the antique prayer book, which stayed in a Paris home until 1991, when the collector's family took it to Christie's for an appraisal, which is where the book's true identity was discovered. Archimedes' journal was appraised at about a million dollars, but sold for more than twice that much at auction in 1998. The anonymous buyer promptly loaned it to the Walters Art Museum in Baltimore, to be deciphered and carefully restored. How many other visionary treatises have vanished? Perhaps as many as the parchment scrolls beneath my sycamore, the caverns in a mountain, or the moments in a day.

The moon disappears behind a wall of sky as the sun flickers through gyrating clouds, creating and just as quickly hiding lit doors into the Civil Morning Twilight. In dawn's misty haze, objects lose their clear edges and the world seems lined with thresholds into the past. I would love to step through one and travel back to the year 1900, near Dunhuang in northern China, where a wandering monk stumbled upon a hidden entrance to a sealed cave in a cliff wall peppered with 492 caves, which locals had been decorating for religious purposes since the fourth century.

For over a thousand years, no wayfarer had paused long enough there to notice anything odd about a too-regular heap of stones. But beneath the stones the monk discovered forty thousand books and manuscripts, written on papyrus and silk scrolls, beautifully preserved by the desert air. A complete library was hidden around A.D. 1000, when the outpost was threatened by invasion from the north. Among the pages wrapped on wooden poles he uncovered the oldest printed book bearing a date, a sixteen-foot woodblock scroll of *The Diamond Sutra*. In a note at the end, a dedication: "Reverently [caused to be] made for universal free distribution by Wang Jie on behalf of his two parents on the thirteenth of the fourth moon of the ninth year of Xiantong [May 11, 868]." Taking about forty minutes to chant, *The Diamond Sutra* teaches that what we see is only an illusion, one created by our brains, which one should cut through with a diamond-like blade. Its final verse says:

So you should view this fleeting world
As a star at dawn, a bubble in a stream,
A flash of lightning in a summer cloud,
A flickering lamp, a phantom, and a dream.

I can't help but wonder about all the other diaries and journals, lovingly kept by earth's kinsmen, that have gone astray, escaped notice, or truly disappeared. *The Diamond Sutra* doesn't suggest denying the world, but first appreciating slippery moments before allowing them to change and melt away. Archimedes' palimpsest offers a spyglass view of our past, another way of knowing that's real as rain and diamond-sharp.

A LITTLE SABBATH WITH
THE SUN

~

I T WAS EASY ENOUGH FOR nomads to chart the travels of
the moon, which could be counted on the fingers. But the
dawn of agriculture, which flourished in the rich river valleys,
required a knowledge of solar time. In Egypt, where the rising
Nile decreed the fate of the crops, astronomers calculated a
365-day solar year as early as 5000–4000 B.C., thousands of
years before the Greeks, Chinese, or Maya. Overlooking the
Mediterranean on Egypt's north shore, the ancient Library of
Alexandria was constructed to receive the sun's first rays on
the summer solstice, when their astrological year and planting
season began.

This was not unusual—we've always built our sacred places
to receive the sun at precisely the moment of spring equinox
or summer solstice. During the reign of Solomon, the Temple
of Jerusalem was oriented to the east, and once a year, on
the spring equinox, the rising sun flashed down a hall to a
small inner sanctuary, which could be entered only by the

high priest. Following the angel of sunlight on that auspicious morning played a key role in the ceremonies. In the city of Thebes, sunlight raced down an avenue into the Great Temple to illuminate the heart of a statue of the sun god. In Celtic burial mounds like Newgrange, built thousands of years before Stonehenge or the Pyramid of Giza, the inner chambers were aligned so that spring's rising sun would sprint the length of a long hall into the deepest chamber, flooding it with light. Harking back to the oldest fertility cults and sun worship, modern European cathedrals and churches—among them Westminster Abbey, St. Paul's Cathedral, Notre Dame in Paris, St. Peter's in Rome, and the Cathedral of Milan—were also oriented to catch the first sun of the first day of spring or summer. Rituals were performed sunwise, as in the Scottish Highland tradition of walking clockwise three times around a person to bless her with good luck. Although the Egyptian priests began shaving circles atop their heads to represent the solar disk, Catholic monks much later adopted the same custom, for reasons now lost to history.

The Library of Alexandria welcomed the sun god in all his manifestations—as a child in spring, an old man in fall, Osiris at sunset, Ra at midday, and Khephera at dawn—and astronomers gathered in its observatory to calculate and record the minutiae of the seasons. In addition to its astronomical observatory and collection of about five hundred thousand scrolls (the equivalent of about thirty thousand modern books), it housed a music school, a philosophical school, and a religious school, as well as thirteen lecture halls with room for five thousand students. What a campus that must have been! The scholars, who rose at dawn for the first classes of the day, learned about the travels of the sun, and awaited their turn to read the original scripts by Aeschylus, Sophocles, and Euripides.

The library was founded during the reign of Ptolemy II, a sun-worshiper, devout celebrant of the dawn, and passionate bibliophile who decreed that every visitor to the city surrender all books, to be immediately copied by scribes. In time, the holdings included every known book of science and literature of its day and all the written knowledge of antiquity. Ringmaster at a court that, for sheer splendor, wit, and excess, rivaled Louis XIV's at Versailles, he also found the energy to collect exotic animals from distant lands, sponsor scientific research, bed a host of brilliant mistresses, and, in his spare time, stage long carnivorous wars, before dying supposedly of "a delicate constitution."

How would Ptolemy have spoken, walked, gestured? He sounds unusually bookish. His childhood tutor was the Alexandrian poet Hilitas of Cos, a leading literary figure, and so Ptolemy would have grown up reading Greek and Latin, at least, reciting poetry by Sappho and others, and wishing to shine in his tutor's eyes. He brokered a deal with the Athenians, borrowing the priceless manuscripts of Greek playwrights, at a steep fee, and had Egyptian scribes copy them. Then he brazenly returned the copies and kept the originals for himself. This infuriated the Greeks, but there's no honor among book thieves, even when they're pharaohs.

Ptolemy is said to have been an avid dawn reader, losing himself in books before the day's statecraft began. I can see him now, robes tinted pink by the low sun over the Nile, sitting in a tree-lined courtyard, beside a pool of lotuses, curled up with a papyrus book.

AUTUMN DAWN

~

MOST OF THE BLOSSOMS HAVE fallen, the burning bushes are blazing scarlet, and they whisper in unison one word: *autumn*. The crozzled old sycamore in the front yard and the magnolia by my bay window still shake bushy heads of green leaves. But slowly, imperceptibly to my eyes, the chlorophyll seeps away for another year, and the smallest dilution of color begins, a little more each hour, each day, until one day, today for instance, I notice a lightening in the forest and the leaf palette beginning to change. They're not cued by the shortening days but by the lengthening nights. Trees can't absorb water from cold soil as fast as it evaporates from their leaves, so to avoid drying out they drop all their leaves. But first they absorb the nutrients, in the process sucking out the green, unmasking the reds and oranges that were there all along. But in big cities, full of artificial light, trees become confused and shed their leaves later in the season. If longer light confuses the trees, what must it do to humans?

Despite the chill, there's still much to treat the senses. At dawn all over America, sunflowers are now turning east and bowing toward the sun. The shaded side of each stem grows faster than the sunny side, and that tilts the flower faces to the light. True believers, they follow the sun during the day, tracking from east to west. A flexible neck below the bud allows the head to turn, but when they bloom, opening into the bright yellow followers that carpet the prairies, the neck stiffens and they're locked in rigid allegiance, most often facing east. A moment ago, instead of "faces," I was going to say "flower," but each sunflower is a throng, not one but a crowd of small florets. All the outer florets are sterile drones, the inner "sunflower seeds" ripe with possibility—another crowd of individuals. The wisdom of the swarm thrives at every level in nature, including our own societies and bodies. Planets gently tug on each other and the sun, which tugs at and is tugged on by other stars in the galaxy, in the process steering their shape and fate. Every *thing* is on the one hand a bundle of characteristics, and on the other all the sensations we feel in its presence. We encounter objects with the whole body, including the object that is the body. Our individual cells combine to boost awareness and build organs and limbs, all of which muster each dawn to reawaken a sense of self. In every neuron and flake of skin, we resemble our one-celled pioneers. More a crowd than a family, our cells are sometimes sociable bedfellows, unknowing companions, secret accomplices. We're really a society of enterprises—breathing, feeding, repairing, moving, planning, maturing. Every body runs millions of tiny factories that, together, coalesce into a self, an *I*, who feels whole, even unique at times, at other times alone. One life emerges. But every *I* is a *we*, a plural event. We compromise, collaborate, sometimes war with ourselves. Most of this is true for other animals as well.

Of course, it's impossible to insert oneself completely into the subjective experience of another person, let alone another species with a different ensemble of senses and instincts. Its day may dawn elsewhere, not with crepuscular rays of sunlight spearing the clouds, but skink-low, or even underground. But there's nothing like the rapture of losing oneself and blending with nature until you can consider the possibility that your molecules might once have been employed elsewhere, in a cuttlefish or a minstrel or a slime mold. It's a humbling thought. We value our own subjective reality above that of any other organism. If we didn't, perhaps we'd feel more kinship with other life-forms, even the lowliest. Consider a being with intelligence, personality, and a gift for learning—despite having no brain whatsoever—the unwittingly resourceful slime mold.

If I were a speck of slime mold, both one and many, a single-celled swarm, a gelatinous glob of peanut butter–like ooze on the forest floor, I would hustle after prey at a flat-out 1 mile per hour, streaming my slime one way, then another, to gobble up bacteria, protozoa, grass, and rotting leaves. Then I might bask on a sunny pile of bark, and jettison a million spores, each to form a single-celled colony of its own, half plant, half animal, all hunger. Self-contained as a solitary regiment, at odd moments I would nonetheless feel a fierce beckoning, unexplained and unshakable, and then I would creep across the ground like a gloved hand to where another slime mold bivouacked. Letting down my walls, I'd surrender my identity and add my society to its, become one hunger, a superorganism with no brain to speak of, but clever and wily, and sublimely temporary, little more than an august mob of cells.

FALSE DAWN

⟞⟋

A GLOWING PYRAMID OF LIGHT ON the horizon tugs at my senses, but it's hours too early for dawn. Also too narrow at only three fists wide, though it stretches halfway up the sky. What is that giant awning of light doing at the edge of the world? This "false dawn," as the twelfth-century Persian poet and astronomer Omar Khayyam called it, is really the *Zodiacal Light*, which fools many dawn-addicts and travelers. Ours is a dusty solar system, full of debris left from the coinage of the planets 4.5 million years ago, and sometimes sunlight, reflecting off millions of seed- to boulder-sized particles orbiting the sun, projects a semblance of dawn in the depths of night. These dust motes glow most when the constellations are at a sharp angle to the horizon; hence their name. Because I'm steeped in darkness, whenever I avert my gaze I catch sight of it at the round eye's so-called corner.

A speck of glitter glides eastward through the stars just above Jupiter and the constellation Scorpio. The *Dawn* spacecraft was launched at sunrise on September 27, 2007, to explore two large pieces of cosmic rubble, dwarf planet Ceres and asteroid Vesta. Its objective is to understand the dawn of the solar system, how the planets formed, and what that implies about planets circling distant stars. During its eight-year mission, it will slingshot around the sun and pause long enough at Vesta and Ceres to orbit, photograph, and measure the two bodies before moving on, never to return home. Like most of our spacegoing vessels, once its dispatches are sent, *Dawn* is slated to travel the oceans of night for eternity, maybe to be recovered one day hundreds or even thousands of years from now, as a message in a bottle from a lonely, curious species.

I am writing this in the tilt of mind we call autumn. How fast it cools in this archipelago of stars, where Earth sails, swollen with fidgeting animals and doubloon-like leaves, the scented ooze of flowers, curtseying geese, jasper bays where whales nurse their young, undersea volcanoes in a petrified seethe, whiz-kid machines, and herds of humans, who speak, love, muse, squabble, and dream. A meteor storm in the forecast. On falling stars thick as fireflies, I wish for brawny atmospheric planets small enough to form oceans and harbor life, where other beings, bustling about their chores, may pause to admire the streaming milt of stars. Maybe, like us, they guide by those nomad lights; maybe they've even named our lantern sun. Other worlds, roll gently around your stars tonight.

NOTHING DOING

I N A DREAM, I'M FLYING above thick heavy storm clouds at dawn into a zone of sunlight with streaks of blue sky and wispy clouds high above. I see a heavy blanket of cloud stretching below me, and under that all of life on earth gyrates. I feel like I'm floating through the non-corporeal mind, floating after death, away from earth, from body, from sensory awareness. After the momentary shivers and terrors comes a sense of freedom. I don't want to return to the storm below. Aloft, all is white, an antarctic vista as far as I can see, white but with dimension: puffs here and there, sinkholes, hills, occasional tints of pale blue smeared across endless pastures of smooth white.

Slowly I become aware that I am in my mother's mind as she was dying seven years ago today, in a hospital I know well, in her mind that had stopped holding on to earth and let itself float, float up through clouds beyond the body, to a realm of sky with blue striations, slowly rising and feeling no senses, no action or activity, yet an awareness of a self floating up out of the self, through the gates of the brain. As her mind began floating away beyond anything like thought, word, or want, a granular white fog moved in, obscuring even the clouds.

Then I realize I am looking at the marbling of the body, the flesh and fluids, seeing from inside the tissues. Looking down, I can feel the body beneath the broken clouds of consciousness, the body with its flowing channels and pastures, its microbial cities and swamps, and dense neural pathways. Then an array of clouds obscures the body, hovering thickly in white ridges and dark gray anvils. We fly right into one surging cloud, become immersed in it, and fly out the other side. Wispier clouds swim across the emptiness like small thought-fish.

Floating somewhere between the body and the mind, I spot a long waterway stretching from north to south, irrigating the lands all around it. Through a hole in the cloud floor I see a wide winding river and miles upon miles of farm fields. Then slowly floating even higher, we enter an area of blue sky and pure yellow sunlight with stray clouds above, and curving all around the bowl of the horizon. The clouds move closer, and I climb knowing that when I pass through them I will enter pure air, pure starlight. It is not so bad parting with the earth. There is great relief.

Life is teeming, anonymous, and disposable. Some religions encourage a loss of self, in essence a glimpse of death during life, with a welcome escape from the struggles of identity. Still, I'm fearful. One is always too young and unready, too polite, too dignified for such radical decay. In this dream the sun blurs the horizon with gold, night and day meet in one quadrant of loss, an indivisible quiet. A heavy white blanket lies below and cloud banks press on the trigger points of morning. Soon we sink between layers in a whiteout bleak as noon on a glacier. Finally, through a long gray coma of clouds, we descend.

I wake up slowly, consciously, trying to remember the softness of my mother's beautiful pale skin, the exact pitch of her upbeat voice, what she looked like as a slender young woman, her changing hairstyles over the years, and as many happy memories of being with her as possible. Not a lot of those memory-twigs exist, unfortunately, and I could use some to nest in now. Marcia died three years after my father Sam. A sense of mourning has been shadowing me for days, the way it sometimes does as her birthday approaches. I've no desire to visit her grave because I believe she's not really there but has rejoined pure energy, once again a shimmer of atoms at dawn. The locals don't say "passed away" but "passed," which sounds a bit more mystical, as in "passed to the other side" or "passed through the veil."

I sense her in the atomic mother-brightening dawn that's glowing chestnut with platinum geysers. I wish our time together had been more intimate, that I'd known more of her dreams and sorrows, understood her better, and that she'd felt known by me. No use fretting over lost possibilities. I hear real peace comes from loving one's fate, not just accepting it, because life is as it is and how one responds is what yields happiness or discontent. Loving your fate without trying to fix it, without asking the universe to be anything it's not, is easier to phrase than to feel, except as desire, and, ironically, the desire itself contradicts the lesson. I find it a state of grace hard to reach. Like trying to frame problems as invitations, not challenges. These fine adjustments echo through the halls of morning.

In Tibetan monasteries, one learns to practice a "death

meditation" at dawn. Upon waking, instead of joining others for sitting meditation and chores, one lies in bed with eyes closed, and says to oneself: *I'm going to die tonight. What shall I do with the rest of my time?* This isn't meant to be a rare occurrence in the otherwise smoothly slathered hours of one's life, but a regular practice over months or years—because it might be true of any day, and certainly will be true one day. Cuddled up with my loving dear? Looking at photographs of my mother? Strolling down the street and feeling the sensations of being alive and in motion? Admiring the beauty of the natural world from sunrise to sunset? Writing a poem? Doing good for the loved ones and others who remain on earth? I begin to appreciate and schedule my allotted hours to what matters most, and that's a tonic to carry into waking life.

The birds start choiring early on, as if they're dragging the sun up to please the Aborigines who dream it with song. A flock of starlings flies over like a pack of noisy children. Yellow-white crystals of sunrise give whatever they strike a brilliant blue luminescence, and it's as if my mother left her awe everywhere for me to find, especially today, lit by the luminol of dawn.

IN THE VASE OF
THE UNIVERSE

⌒

"COME QUICKLY. YOU MUSTN'T MISS the dawn!" Geor-
gia O'Keeffe once urged her guests at her Abiquiu, New
Mexico, house in 1951. "It will never be just like this again!!"

As I set out for a walk, stalks of pink and orange clouds
rise straight up in a porcelain-blue sky. Is the sky a blue vase?
Only as part of the vase of the universe, mottled with planets,
surging with broths and possibly with other planetarians who
quest and question. A good walk, despite the pinched nerves
in my neck, which I've been suffering with sometimes might-
ily, anxiously, despairingly, maybe even angrily (Angri-la, that
paradise of rage in the Himalayas of the mind). I've felt volumes of suffering during these days, but not unhappiness. I love
being part of the saga of life on earth, and both suffering and
change feature large in that adventure, *are* that adventure. For
the moment, we can only know Earth-life, the shape and com-
plexion life has found in us and our neighbors, on the home
planet where we were born. It's ironic that we designate this or

that landform as a natural wonder, when no facet of nature is
as unlikely as we, the tiny bipeds with the giant dreams. I mean
our being here at all, given all the twists, turns, sidesteps, leaps,
and genetic bottlenecks of evolution. We are natural wonders,
creatures easy to know, but hard to know well.

Low in the sky, a floury white sun floats in a ring of its
yellow gases. St. Francis is said to have rung the church bells
during the night, and when the villagers gathered to ask about
the emergency, he said: "Lift up your eyes! Look at the moon!"
A bright, baying moon hangs low this morning over the tall
grasses and the black-eyed Susans beloved by the quick chit-
tering goldfinches that lunge and fall in flight.

The voracious cicadas prefer the oak, hickory, and apple
trees growing abundantly in my yard. But the trees fight back
with their own chemistry labs and arsenals. There's nothing
mild-mannered about plants, which don't just lure insects
and other pollinators to their combination espresso bar and
opium den. Some compel them. Since plants don't travel much,
they've become clever assassins and wily suitors, devising inge-
nious ways for other animals to help them have sex.

Consider the innocent-looking milkweed in my yard, an
aggressive lothario with slippery flowers that grab an insect's
legs. Then bees and flies are treated to pollen britches on their
way out. A female monarch butterfly (soft white-speckled belly
and no spots on her wings) hovers above the milkweed, lands
on a blossom which she grips with tenterhook feet, and unrolls
her party-favor tongue.

A landing moth slides around until its feet get caught in
tiny pollen-coated clamps that attach yellow sacs. Struggling to
pull free, it lifts one leg, now wearing a pollen saddlebag, then
another. At least the moth exits. Fine debris on the flower tells

the tale of some insects that weren't lucky enough to escape. As the moth travels to other plants, it will deposit some of the pollen and the rest will eventually fall as part of a wasteful harum-scarum system that works.

Newly opened milkweed pods offer bunches of seeds with silken parachutes designed to travel far. Monarch butterfly caterpillars, feeding on the leaves, flavor themselves with enough poison to use as chemical body armor. But cooking disarms the poison. Chefs sometimes prepare the spring shoots like asparagus, the unopened buds like broccoli florets, the flowers battered and fried, the early pods boiled in several waters to subdue the bitter "milk." Sweet flowers can be stewed and eaten like jam, the early pods fried like okra. Orioles tug fibers from the milkweed stems to brace their nests. The delirium of milkweed silk used to provide peasants with stuffing for pillows and beds, or the silk could be mixed with flax or wool and woven into thread. It took about nine pounds of silk for a mattress. In World War II, milkweed down was used in life preservers and to line airmen's uniforms. Harvesters collected the dry pods when they were bursting with silk, which is nothing more (or less) than millions of tiny tubes filled with air.

All I mean to do with this milkweed is admire it and remember my mother, one of its great devotees, who always graced our living room with a vase of milkweed pods, some closed, others spilling their silk. In her last years, I sometimes collected milkweed from the fields and culverts for her. She needed to have some pods with her everywhere she lived, I'm not sure why, and now it's too late to ask her. Were they a memory aid to carefree days as a girl on Maryland's Eastern Shore? Did they suggest hidden selves held captive inside a familiar husk?

She would have liked knowing that whenever one sees milkweed, a mother plant with long runners is sprouting off-spring underground, below the consciousness of air. In that down-reaching world, milkweed leads a different life, locking horns with such foes as mice, star-nosed moles, and rot. It keeps its hungers separate—sex aboveground, food below—and spreads fast into a pillow fight of many pod-laden plants. But every *it* is a *we*, all one family sprouting up from a single runner, in their roots and deepest strivings still attached to mother.

Every autumn my garden also becomes a booby trap of mole holes, a maze of tunnels trailing just below the surface. I've never seen any of the moles, crouch as I might behind rosebushes at dawn, since they don't emerge for breakfast, but mainly feed on earthworms and other invertebrates that stray into the tunnels, which act as snares The soil in my garden is too acidic to support the feast of earthworms moles might find in a sunny meadow, but it only takes a few moles to riddle the ground, as one mole's territory can be 700 square yards with six levels of tunnel. They create shallow tunnels by pushing into the soil and stiffening the body to strengthen the walls. Come autumn, the moles excavate more, I presume because as the soil grows colder earthworms must tunnel deeper (and moles in pursuit). For deep tunnels a mole digs up the soil behind it, somersaults, then pushes the loose dirt aboveground, creat-ing the famous molehill in the process. That takes so much time and toil that it's earned them the collective term of a *labor* of moles. In breeding season, February and March, moles risk leaving their territories to look for mates, but otherwise they're mainly hermits who chase away intruders. Dauntless male moles, who pound their heads against tunnel ceilings to entice females, might be head-drumming right now. Listening hard, I don't hear them, but it amuses me to know they're underfoot wildly thumping come-hithers.

Lots of dead bees in the pool. These "watermaid" bees collect water from swimming pool, pond, and puddle, carrying it home to toss onto the hot hive, where the water evaporates and cools the queen, even when the temperature starts to fall in autumn. It's hard not to picture them lugging tiny buckets.

In the front courtyard beneath a hanging fuchsia is a white scrawl I recognize as slime left by a slug. In the driveway I find hopscotch and free-form chalk drawings. Worms lie on the road, one coiled into a question mark. These three have nothing in common, except as designs created by living things, but the pattern-mad brain links them, just in case the similarity may matter one day when the stakes are higher.

Carefully raked piles of red, orange, and yellow leaves line the roadway. Sometimes the whole world seems to be shedding its previous selves. Not just the local deer and squirrels, but the garter snakes and foxes. We shed our top layer of skin every two weeks, and every fall the birches strew the ground with bark, a pageant I find pretty and scroll-like, but birds put to clever use.

As the sun drives gold nails into the shadows, a red-winged blackbird lands near the sycamore, pecks at a tatter of bark, then ruffles its feathers, cranes its neck, and curries its chest feathers with gusto. Another peck at the bark litter. The bird waddles in place. Another spirited rub, this time under one wing. Another peck. Twisting its chest like a lid, it aims to reach back feathers, jabbing at them several times. And so the cycle of poses continues, a sort of feathered tai chi.

At last the red-winged flies off, and I can inspect the ground where it danced. There fifty or so alarmed ants still scramble, and some lie twitching and injured. The blackbird was "anting," an avian habit of squeezing an ant until it sprays formic acid, an irritant used to curb enemies and prey. Anointing its feathers with this caustic bath helps the red-winged control parasites, so anting is hygienic, but birds can become so addicted to it that when ants are scarce they'll use orange peels, mothballs, cigarette ash, walnut husks, lemons, bombardier beetles, and even beakfuls of smoke. Honeybees make their own formic acid to kill mites in the hives, and we humans sometimes add it to livestock feed to curb bacteria.

Many animals use nature's apothecary. Starlings sanitize their nests with sprigs of herbs. I've seen capuchin monkeys rub themselves with millipedes as an insecticide, lathering on some millipede juice and then passing the bug along to a neighbor as if it were a bottle of Cutter's repellent. Brown lemurs use dill weed to keep mosquitoes at bay. In Tanzania, chimpanzees sometimes eat the leaves of the shrub *Trichilia rubescens*, which has anti-malarial properties; and they chew on the pith inside the stems of a plant known as *bitter leaf* to cure intestinal ills, just as the local Tongwe people do. I recently heard a Kenyan's story about hunters pursuing a small group of elephants and shooting a large bull. As it lay dying, the other elephants began hurriedly packing the wound with mud. Wild camels, colobus monkeys, chimpanzees, and other animals forage for charcoal left by fires to eat as a remedy for poisons. Wounded animals— from elk to bears—roll in clay, or dip a limb in freezing water to speed healing or staunch bleeding. Deer rub their wounds against sweet gum trees, whose resin is antiseptic. In fact, so many wild animals use medicines that there's a field of study devoted to it: zoopharmacognosy.

In my cruel and heartless days, before I appreciated the sleek beauty of garden slugs, I put out bowls of beer for slugs to crawl into and drown. Unfortunately, raccoons would find the bowls at night, eat the beer-basted slugs, and get drunk; it became their tapas bar. But I once saw a blue jay spritzing itself with the beer. If that sounds peculiar, consider this: we rub ourselves with pungent ooze from the anal sacs of civets, gargle with peppermint oil, and spritz ourselves with pig pheromone in order to attract mates. That's equally strange. And for all I know, there may also be humans who ant.

There's nothing like a fall sky to snatch the wool of familiarity away from my eyes. The intricate twigs and branches of leafless trees cage the pale blue—a crystalline sky—and the weeping willows weep at their most beautiful, with cherry-brown bark full of gnarls and bulges that create faces. Dry leaves, fallen onto the dark road, glow like golden minnows. It's cool this morning, in the low 40s and misty, with here and there a white rainbow, a *mistbow*. The air stretches my nostrils and my mind utters *smoke, wood, chimney fire*, and pictures a man bending at a hearth to agitate the luminous coals.

The trees, the streetlamps, the doe with a tag in her ear, the houses, the worms that unsaddle to mate—how strange, how wonderful to be a part of this flutter in the eye of the cosmos, this tiny planet that spawned life. Here only this once and never again, I want to stop ten times a day, stop whatever I'm saying or doing, and behold the human pageant with its uncountable dramas, step back and marvel that life evolved, the shapes and strategies it pursues, marvel at how possessed people stay, by choice, with feats of distraction and the rigors of daily life, willingly spellbound, racing to life's end.

Where several driveways meet the road, short brown sen-

tries squat: bags of raked leaves, with *True Value* printed in bold
red letters. Garbage that's true value? It seems a contradiction,
except perhaps to draw our attention to what passes for value,
and the beauty we reject just because it has aged and fallen.
Finally I arrive at a glowing yellow street sign announcing DEAD
END. We come to this knowledge late, most people not until the
end of their life, when, like my mother, they say wistfully, more
lament than comment, the genuinely felt mystery: "Where did
the time go?" It seems only poetic that the woodpeckers love
to peck at the yellow sign, drumming their whereabouts, claim,
and desire to all comers on a rusty metal sun.

CLEVER AS CLEVER

Seventeen
starlings on the telephone wire . . .
sixteen

—GEORGE SWEDE

IN A MOONLESS SKY, JUPITER glows like a small twist of hot wire. But in my mind I see it the way it looks in photographs, complete with stripes and a colossal red storm cloud scouring its face. Dawn wells up, as if the ground were oozing light, the air brightens into blue, and suddenly inkblots rip through on wings. Few things are as beautiful as these huge clouds of starlings swooping and whirling around a milky blue sky at dawn. They echo the undulations of Florida's collared doves, except that they vastly outnumber them and most other American birds.

As the rising sun glitters off the golden speckles among their feathers, a string of starlings roosts on the wires. The score they compose this morning is:

I've always liked crowds of starlings, maybe because they remind me that all humans today descended from a small tribe of clever talkative people who survived a planet of ice. That bottleneck might have included only thirty or so child-bearing women. Life always begins small, homesteads a patch of earth, ocean, or sky, and as it grows pioneers the wildest unknowns.

This population of starlings started small, too. A tweed delight to some and a pest to others starlings aren't native to North America, but very recent immigrants. In March 1890, Eugene Schieffelin, a New York drugmaker, released the first hundred in Central Park as part of a gift from a bird-loving Shakespearean society that wanted to fill the landscape with the songbirds mentioned in Shakespeare's plays.

A robust species, the European starling crossed the Mississippi River by 1929, and today tens of millions of starlings nest in the spring, and then form giant flocks of up to 150,000 in the fall and winter—known as *murmurations* or *chatters* of starlings. At this time of year, starlings roost in backyard evergreens, with the oldest birds in the center, and the rest changing position during the night, depending on how cold they're feeling. Now I'm blinded by the sunlamp right behind their wires—all I hear is their raucous clamor, a nut-cracking sound I've come to cherish.

At sunrise, they scatter to hunt in small flocks across the landscape, and I've sometimes seen them perching around chimneys to keep warm. I watch their morning forays, and wait to see if they'll visit my yard for grubs and berries. I like how their powerful jaw muscles work backward, allowing them to open their bills forcefully, instead of clamping tight. It's an odd trait, which they use for prying open seeds and fruits, and sometimes they spear the soil and spring open their bills to expose prey. But it might also help with speech.

Members of the myna family, they're legendary mimics of everything from hawks to hammers, and tame starlings learn to talk and sing *human* as well as *starling*. Starlings in the Shetland Islands *baah* across the hillsides with the sheep, and in some cities they mimic buses. According to Pliny the Elder, Romans commonly taught starlings to echo Greek and Latin and the birds "practiced diligently and spoke new phrases every day, in still longer sentences."

I have a friend, Kyllikki, whose three-year-old starling, Sprinkle, has an unusually large vocabulary, which leads to a fizzy stream of babbling. Sprinkle mixes nonsense words with real words, and since she lives in a big house with a parrot and a myna bird (as well as two cats), one often hears her chitchat parroted back. She's partial to rhyme, whether it makes sense or not. When my physician friend Ann and I were visiting the other day, she rhymed "stomach" with "fromach."

Sprinkle talks to herself nonstop whenever she's playing alone or bored, and since she likes to watch doctor shows on TV, the babble occasionally includes words like "esophagus," "pertussis," or "ligaments." I'm impressed by her good grammar. Not only does she utter complete sentences, with all the words in the right order, she makes up words and uses them correctly.

For instance, when Kyllikki gave her a mealworm and asked if she liked it, Sprinkle said:

"It's Sprinklicious."

At one point Ann and I were distracted by an avant-garde artwork on the fireplace mantel, an old-fashioned toaster jazzed up with colorful decorations. Towering above the starling's cage, I would have thought we were well out of earshot as we discussed the offbeat creation.

"Obsolete toaster," Sprinkle suddenly piped up.

Well, that floored me. "Obsolete toaster?" I repeated.

"Sprinkle's smart," she said, and cackled a long, hearty laugh. Her laugh triggered a bout of echolalia. The more she laughed we laughed, the more we laughed she laughed, and her owner laughed at all three of us.

I guess Sprinkle thought Ann and I looked—or maybe sounded—alike, because a few days later we heard from Kyllikki that Sprinkle had guessed we were "sisters from Trumansburg," a nearby town.

A precocious three-year-old can be mighty clever and hazard endless guesses, and do some abstract thinking, even if she isn't potty-trained. But a starling? Let me tell you it's hilarious, when the housecat passes her cage, to hear Sprinkle call out mischievously: "Here, kitty, kitty."

As I've now been informed by people in starling-friendly households, starlings are the grammarians of the bird world. Instead of echoing one or two words, they like rhythmic phrases and whole sentences, and often include nonverbal sounds, too, like sneezing or the owner's wheeziness or cough. It's hard to know which words might catch a starling's fancy. Human language being as suggestive as it is, when Sprinkle gives a phrase different inflections it can sound insightful. A starling's "I'll say good morning!" has a different effect when she clips the phrase to "I'll say!" Sprinkle's sentences mutate, and she often engages in what we would call simple conversation:

Kyllikki (about the pet goldfish): "All goldfish are beautiful. Are all starlings beautiful?"

Sprinkle: "*I'm* pretty."

Kyllikki: "Sprinkle has a beautiful beak. I don't have a beak."

Sprinkle: "You can borrow my beak."

Kyllikki sometimes logs Sprinkle's chatter, which includes such surprises as: "Allow me to take control!" and "You are said to be bald and armless . . . that's *unusual*." Here's one soliloquy, and it's typical, except that it continued all day:

"You're such a Barbie! . . . Did you see my beautiful beak? My lips are sealed. . . . It's luminous. . . . Please allow me a small bunch of nematodes. . . . Sprinky loves fish, they all say kiss . . . amethysts, halitosis. . . . You lied to me about sparrows! . . . shaving beaks . . . terrorists! . . . Is that a good purse? . . . Allow me to be ashamed. . . . My beak's a frazzle! . . . I like fools who stand on tippy-toes . . . shmatta! . . . You're a good sport. . . . The fish have a business. . . . I'm at that point in my life. . . . You are a good girl. . . . You make me miserable. . . . Aren't you nice. . . . I'm getting dressed. . . . I like shoe trees . . . contagious, outrageous. . . . A mister is like a sister, hahaha . . ."

One day, when Kyllikki's husband called upstairs, "What are you doing?" and Kyllikki answered, "Brushing my teeth," the starling chimed in: "Not invasive surgery!"

On a January morning, Kyllikki opened her blinds to find a spotlight sun blasting over the sill and pouring buckets of yellow marbles through the grass. "Isn't it beautiful?" she exclaimed. To which Sprinkle replied: "Oy vey, it's beautiful."

I don't know what Sprinkle makes of the dawn, only that it wakes her, even indoors, because starlings instinctively disperse from their night roost at sunrise, and I wonder if she feels a tugging to join the circling flock silhouetted against the sun. Like cranes, starlings learn how to flock from older adults. But the ability to create sentences, and expand them by inserting correct words and clauses, once thought to be a uniquely human specialty, comes naturally to her. She can even do embedded grammar, so "Oedipus ruled Thebes," can become "Oedipus, who killed his father, ruled Thebes," or "Oedipus, who killed his father, whom he met on the road from Delphi, ruled Thebes," and so on. But despite Sprinkle's combinative gusto, starlings usually don't generalize from patterns the way we do, which leaves us alone to invent false teeth and explore other planets.

I'm sure Sprinkle's verbal finesse comes from a dynamic relationship with her adoptive mother, Kyllikki. The social life of wild starlings includes forging strong bonds with family members whom they mimic and try to please. When Sprinkle was only a few days old, she was pushed out of her nest (most likely by a rival sibling), and Kyllikki found the floppy hatchling and began raising it indoors in a very verbal household.

Mozart once kept a pet starling that liked to pipe along with his music, and some say he returned the compliment by weaving starling tunes into his compositions. Over three years, he grew very attached to the bird he called "Jester" or "Clown." Unfortunately, he didn't know that starlings eat insects and worms in the wild and require a varied diet of fruits, vegetables, and protein. He meant well by feeding it good bread, but in time it died, to Mozart's deep sorrow. Mourning, he devised an elaborate funeral for the bird (and, if you're of a Freudian turn of mind, for his father, who died the same week). Friends were asked to attend in funeral attire, and were expected to sing hymns to the departed. At the graveside, Mozart recited an elegiac poem he'd written. Many musicologists argue that the score he composed a week later (*Musical Joke*, K. 522)—full of starling rhythms, rambling, disjointed sounds, and aural pranks—was a tribute to his beloved Jester.

FIELD GUIDES

⌒

Dawn is storming in, racing a drizzly blue light across the sky. One crow unlocks the morning with a simple *caw, caw, caw, caw.* It sounds irritable, even for a crow call, which can scrape the ears with the likes of: *I'm up, dammit. I'm up! I survived another night on this godforsaken planet! Beat that!* It reminds me that a mass of crows is called a *murder* of crows.

As Earth rolls through shorter days, the trees twitch with young birds far from nest or knothole, some still being supported by their parents. A new red-winged blackbird lands hard in the sycamore, then does the fluff-and-quiver dance that means *Feed me!* Moments later its mother arrives, back-flapping into a perfect stall, holding a green tidbit in her beak. She shoves it into the fledgling's gaping mouth.

A gray cat sits at the edge of a crescent flower bed, blending in beside a plastic owl of about the same size. The bobble-head owl was designed to scare deer away from the daylilies but a doe kicked its head off, which I believe earned her access to the flowers. Now the cat silently glides into a better position, camouflaged by leaves and shade. As a rabbit hops into view by the garden gate, the cat crouches like a sphinx and freezes, fixated. When the unsuspecting rabbit strays to within four yards of it, the cat springs into motion, bolts into the backyard, and returns a moment later, lugging the rabbit in its mouth. I gasp and the cat hears me, startled just a flinch long enough for the rabbit to squirm free and dart away with the cat in swift pursuit. Half a minute later the cat slouches back through the underbrush, empty-jawed.

A brightening. Drowsy well-fed owls will be settling in to sleep, maybe tucking nests full of chicks beneath their embracing wings. I keep wondering about the large white stain high up on a hickory, just beneath a stubby branch, a good perch for surveying the backyard. It looks like guano—bird or bat, and whatever left it was big and perched for a long time. I hope it's an owl that settles there each night, fifty feet up, to survey the yard for its dining pleasure. I saw an eastern screech owl in silhouette one evening, sitting in the branches of a tree. I knew him by the ear tufts and bowling-bag body, but it was too dark for me in the closing rounds of dusk to make out his amber eyes. See me? He would have read every line on my face, every eyelash. I don't know if he understood about reflection, or the removable exoskeletons of our cars, or regarded our houses as giant nests built for us by others using tree wood and unidentifiable gubbins. But I'm a big fan of owls.

I would be an owl if I could, an *ule*, a creature named after its sound. So I would be a howl if I could, sweet cheat of the night, who slices open the air with soft serrated wings, so silently I don't warn dozy prey. How far can I see? An owl could read the bottom line on an eye chart from a mile off, or hear a mouse stepping on a twig seventy-five feet away. Tuning and retuning, I would be an owl with ears twin radar dishes, eyes winged binoculars. A screech owl because, though baby screechers screech, the adults make the most enchanting soft whinnying-howl. Owl of the stethoscope ears.

I'd swallow meals whole, headfirst, tumbling soft and furry down my throat to the fiery plant that compacts all the inedibles into a hard pellet. Twice a day, growing bloated and queasy, I'd stretch my neck up and forward, squeeze my stomach hard, and vomit a hairy bony nugget. Oh, I'd vomit gently, all things considered, not thrash and shake the pellet free for five minutes like other inversely constipated owls. I'd eagerly coax these dainty pukes. Not like the giant sea cucumber that hurls up its whole stomach and tosses it, literally, at the missing feet of a wall-eyed fish, then, while the distracted fish feasts, steals away, a gutless wonder but alive, soon to grow another stomach.

I'd sing of owl-puke, the pellets that pave my days with dense nuggets that offer home to fungi, beetles, and other tramps. Does it sound nicer as a fur ball? I suppose it does. But a little cat fur swallowed while grooming can't compare to a stony wadded-up girdle of rodent, shrew, mole, gecko, and snake skeleton, mixed with beetle crackle and songbird wings and oily fur, as if for a jigsaw puzzle of a chimera, part mammal, part bird, part reptile, part insect, all tasty.

Yes, all things considered, I would be an *ule* with a ukelele call, a cowl of gray feathers cupping my feathered jowls, talons sharp and strong as ice hooks, parachute wings, a demisuit of down, *ule*-tide duels, and ingenue eyes, voodoo eyes. I would be possessed of the ultimate head swivel: upside down and around back and front again over the other shoulder. Hunting among oaks and cottonwoods and old shady maples, with broad wings outstretched and head tucked in tight, I'd flap hard and fast, rarely gliding or hovering, while listening and watching for scuffling prey in the leaf litter and lawns.

I'd sing duets with my mate during the day and be calmed by a male chorus at night, a *parliament* of owls. What a panoply of songs and calls! The territorial flute-and-glass-bell tune, *This is my land*; the chortling duet of *food bringing*; the descending whinnies of courtship; the *Here comes the sun!* and *Night is falling* hoots; the reassuring *I'm bringing food home* hoot; the happy *pottering around the nest* hum; the scratchy alarm call; the faint but strident begging calls of the young; the explosive *Get off my land!* barks uttered in flight; the throaty trills while gabbing with a mate; the defensive hoots and harangues at nest invaders; and the billboard-loud advertising song, *Look no further, I'm one hell of an owl!*

When frightened, I'd blend in with tree trunk or foliage, stretching my frame long, closing my eyes to slits, tightening my feathers, and standing still as old bark. In winter, I'd gobble hot meals of warm-blooded prey, and in summer cool crisp lizards, snakes, and bugs. And it goes without saying that I would marry for life, a long life of a score or two, lengthened by living in the suburbs and devouring the rat race.

I would be an owl with wide feather skirts to curtsy with when courted by bowing suitors. Oh, the formal dances of courtship, ceremonial and piquantly Oriental. First a spring-time male calls, robust as all get out, and I reply, we flirt like this several times, then I see him flying in, watch him perch nearby, and begin head-bobbing and bowing deeply, repeat-edly, now and then winking one eye. Ignore him and he just

chases harder. Accept, and the bill kissing and mutual preening begins, with the preened one uttering soft whimperings
of delight, both fine-feathered friends amused and enthused.
Yes, all things considered, I would be an *ule*, with owl-bright
eyes, creature comforts, and wide wings with down fur below
to wrap my chicks in owl love.

WINTER

WHERE IT'S WINTER

～

WHEN THE SEINE FROZE SOLID in the winter of 1892–93 and then thawed, Monet painted the series *Ice-Floes*, a startling landscape of pastel ice afloat on glassy silvery-gray-to-gold water. Some of the whitest whites exist as bare canvas he decided not to paint. Monet understood the subjective lens through which snow, though rumored to be white, often appears confetti-colored as it reflects the winter sun. Dig a hole in the snow and a blue shadow appears at the bottom, because on our planet all shadows are blue, sky-tinted, the scheme of winter dawn.

An opalescent sky becomes the stinging blue of mosque tiles or stage scenery. It's an *azure* blue, from the ancient word for lapis lazuli, the intense blue mineral flecked with gold that has emblazoned church and palace walls since antiquity. Polished lapis gives soul to a mosaic, including dawn's chimeras of jumbled outlines, blurred edges, and phantom forms. We bundle up but trees go naked in winter. I've always loved the way sky is captured in their bare limbs. Held by the delicate tracery of twigs, sky resembles light pouring through leaded stained-glass windows.

A full moon in the western sky glows the same size, color, and brightness as a streetlamp, and for nocturnal animals and night-navigating humans it serves the same old purpose. Suddenly, like silent reveille, the smoky blue whitens until individual seedpods become visible and also human presence. The moon shadows evaporate like invisible ink. Night's illusions retire as day's illusions prosper.

Then the sun rises like a pale yellow ghost.

An icy morning. Frail crunching underfoot sounds like ducks quacking. In cold air, the brittle crystals smash together, losing their starfish-like arms in the collisions, and become hard crunchy snow. What I like about crusty snow is that you can always tell who's been around. Though it carves and packs well for snow forts, it's difficult to walk on, and so instead of trailing their legs as they do in powdery snow, the deer leave individual pockets where they step. In the excitement before dawn today, birds etched hieroglyphics, deer ran swiftly parallel to the front walk, and a dog settled for a moment under the patio table before making tracks toward the woods.

Floating through warmer air, the first snows of winter build the largest flakes, each one a mat of hundreds of crystals bumping together and sticking as they fall. I love watching finches, ravens, and other birds bathing in fluffy snow, and playing in it, too, rolling around and sliding down snow piles. Sometimes an *unkindness* of ravens will gather for snow play, or a *scolding* of jays. Today every branch, roof, birdhouse, and car is crusted high. Snow speckles the ground and follows the natural shape of things: frosting mounds over the globe lights above the mailbox,

lying flat on the square birdhouse, and sprinkling the tops of
the magnolia branches. One broken hickory looks like a statue
of Liberty: uplifted arm, gray bosom, flowing bark robes.

I put most of the rosebushes to bed for the winter before the
first snowfall and freeze. Some remain to mound with several
feet of mulch, topped by a layer of fallen leaves, topped by an
icing of insulating snow. It's odd to think of snow keeping
things warm, but the crystal blanket both chills what it touches
and insulates what lies beneath, shielding plants or arctic hunters from icy winds. So I wrapped some bushes in chicken wire
before the layering began, and now the yard looks like a cityscape with dozens of elfin chimneys. Porch lights shine along
the street—white, yellow, gold—like distant stars each tinted
differently by the gas at its core. As a result shadows streak
behind the trees. The magnolia branches are all elbows.

Winter is a blue season, gray-blue at dawn, blue-white in
landscapes, and for many people blue in mood. For them it's
not enough that the sun rises each day, if it just trickles copper
across the lake instead of trumpeting reds and oranges. The
short days don't fill their reservoirs of light, and anyway most
of the animals are scarce and the plants dead. Personally, I love
winter, and regard snow as a great big toy that falls from the
sky, just as I did as a child. I love how snow becomes a prism
in the sun, crinkling with colors, and how ice coating a wire
fence creates visual firecrackers. I love that snow is a mineral,
falling as billions of temporary stars.

Today I am paging through an exquisite atlas of snowflakes,
from crystal ferns and side-branching stars edged with rime
droplets to ice slabs and puffball clusters. They're not all sym-
metrical. Some sport tails and daggers, twelve-sided wheels, or
stinging needles; others show hourglass hollows inside.

In 1637, René Descartes, philosopher and naked-eye devotee of snowflakes, wrote my favorite description of them in *Les Météores*: "After this storm cloud, there came another, which produced only little roses or wheels with six semicircular teeth." And in the winter of 1856, Henry David Thoreau saw a lovely meteor shower in a snowstorm: "How full of the creative genius is the air! I should hardly admire them more if real stars fell and lodged on my coat."

But it was "the Snowflake Man," Wilson A. Bentley, a petite mustache-adorned nineteenth-century farmer from Jericho, Vermont, who dreamt up snow-crystal photography and the first album of snowflakes. In his teens, Bentley peered at snowflakes through a microscope and spent monk-like hours sketching their forms. That led him to the avid microphotography of snowflakes in auspicious weather—preferably 20 to 25 degrees Fahrenheit—"out in a shed or lean-to, with the camera pointed toward an open door," a visitor recalled, "so that the illumination would pass through the snow crystal." A self-described confirmed bachelor, Bentley occupied one wing of the large old family farmhouse he shared with his nephew, whose wife was forbidden ever to enter or clean his lodgings. As a result, he lived in less-than-snowflake order in a small bedroom, with a piano that "showed an arc from treble to bass where his fingers in playing had cleared dust from the keys, while beyond the reach of his fingers the dust was banked between the black keys and into the corners." His hands were callused and knotty from work on his dairy and fruit farm, which supported the clarity of his hours staring into the vanishing faces of ice crystals. In 1931, he caught pneumonia while traveling home from a lecture through a severe snowstorm, but he had to go home, his host reported, "because the storm was the type that yielded a certain sort of snow crystal that he wanted!" A seminal book about snowflakes, including two thousand of his best photographs, was in production at a publishing house when he died. A shame. He would have been able to hold a permanent blizzard in his hands, snowflakes that never melted. By that time he had gained worldwide fame as the Snowflake Man, his photographs adorned the official National Weather Bureau calendars, and he had launched an idea that quickly gained status as a powerful metaphor: no two snowflakes are alike.

A winter morning in northern latitudes: pale blue snow highlights the angle of each roof. Two dry leaves swoop and flutter like moths. A lone doe ambles down the street, like any other neighbor on her way to work. No doubt she has already foraged in my yard. I leave plants around the front of the house for the deerfolk to browse, because this small parcel of land was theirs before it was mine, and I feel a little guilty about the fencing in and doling out of what once flowed seamlessly from forest to gorge. Home is where the heart is, we say, rubbing the flint of one abstraction against another. A house can be a simple shelter, but *home* is the carapace of one's inner life. Heavily idealized, it includes a foundation, insulation, and all the right tools for every real or imaginary calamity.

With the roads too snowy to bike on today, I may swim at the Y if my knee permits. Sometimes the deer also have leg problems, despite their muscle tone, given their slender legs and narrow ankles. Built like racehorses, they balance heavy muscle on petite anklebones and it's a surprise to me that their legs don't fail them more often. The bone wings of the pelvis evolved in many mammals to spare the backbone and legs pain, and by and large that system works for the first years of maturity, a reproductive Valhalla. After that, it's every human, deer, elephant, and roebuck for itself. How fitting that the Elizabethans called the body the "bone house." My knee, neck, and back all are griping me today. I know there's at least a knee replacement in my future. One has to laugh. Over the years I've had to make many repairs to my home in upstate New York; why did I think it would be any different with the bone house?

WATER, WATER EVERYWHERE

⌒

The eye, when it opens, is like the dawn breaking
in the night . . . a new world is there.

—JOHN O'DONOHUE, ANAM CARA

IN THE SAPPHIRE HOURS BEFORE sunrise, ice floes on the
lake crack the mirror reflection of trees. Elsewhere in town,
waterfalls tumble and spume in lofty dialects of water. Icy
scarves loop through glacier-carved gorges, and winter reminds
us that light airy bits of water can hurdle fences, collapse buildings, and bring a burly city to its knees. On this blue winter
morning, ice forms a cataract on the eye of Lake Cayuga, and
milky tusks adorn the inlet, but the whole lake never freezes
solid. It can't.

Luckily for us. Eccentric right down to our atoms, we'd be
impossible without water's weird bag of tricks. The litany of
we're only here because begins with this chilling one: We're only
here because ice floats. Other liquids contract and sink when
they freeze, but water alone expands, in the process growing
minute triangular pyramids that clump to form spacious, holey
designs that float free. If ice didn't rise, the oceans would have

frozen solid long ago, along with all the wells, springs, and rivers. Without this presto chango of water, an element that one moment slips like silk through the hands and the next collapses rooftops and chisels gorges, Earth would be barren.

Since life bloomed in the seas, we need perpetual sips of fresh water to thrive. Become dehydrated, as I once did in Florida, and the brain's salt flats dry out, mental life dulls, and only electrolytes dripped into a vein keep death at bay. We are walking basins, who quaff water and also bathe in it, irrigate with it, paddle through it, simmer with it, and are rained on by it, so we rarely notice how magical water is. Water can be liquid, vapor, crystal. Though water often looks like glass, and in some brittle forms can shatter like glass, and in others flow thick and slow as glass, it's not made of silica as glass is. But it does sponsor glass. The sandy skirts edging some oceans are a form of glass crafted by water.

No water is new. Endlessly levitating, falling, and condensing, every drop is recycled from somewhere and somewhen else. The water in today's stalk of celery may have dropped as rain in the Amazon last year, or fed an African well three million years ago. We've learned how to catch and carry water, but not, alas, precisely where we may wish. Half of the world's rain showers down on the Amazon, falling thick as rubber, a place where I once walked through an eerie veil of 100 percent humidity that wasn't raining.

Covering half of the planet, clouds look collaged onto the sky, Rorschach-like nomads that collapse and descend as rain. But they do not move through the air, they *are* air, minute droplets so light they're carried on the wind. Thousands of tons of water, millions of drops, they look serene but are unstable, jostling hordes. Who could begin to classify them?

No one dared until 1802, when French naturalist Jean-Baptiste Lamarck sorted clouds as: *hazy, massed, dappled, broom-like,* or *grouped.* Soon afterward British pharmacist Luke Howard proposed the four classes of *cumulus, stratus, nimbus,* and *cirrus,* which we haven't revised much except to add the altitude, as in the rippling pink and white bands of *altocumulus* on display right now.

Aerial water can't compete with the oceans for sheer volume, of course, but snowmelt and rain replenish lakes and rivers, springs and wells, and abounding life-forms, including six billion humans. I may say and think humans walk, but what we really do is flow. When we lie down like spirit levels, our waters flatten, but they keep moving, sliding, gliding, renewing. Even inactive folk end up travel-stained after a while, thanks to the body's aqueducts and navies. Drinking, eating, excreting, and thinking water, our tissues are marshes and estuaries, our organs islands, our bloodstreams long rivers with creeks and feeders. Sloshing sacs of chemicals on the move, we leak from many orifices throughout our life and still carry the salty ocean in our blood, skin, sweat, and tears. Menstrual periods mirror the tides. We need water to oil joints, digest food, build the smile-bright enamel on our teeth. We are water's way of reflecting on the life it promotes.

Because we're mostly water ourselves, surrounded by water, we *go with the flow, water down* proposals, *spend money like water,* have *liquid assets, dilute* drinks, *take the plunge,* go through *baptisms of fire,* try not to be *shallow.* Past events we banish as *water under the bridge.* Gushing out alive after nine months afloat, we nonetheless fear death by water, fear *getting in over our heads,* until we're *drowning* in work, *flooded* by emotion, and flailing just to keep our *heads above water,* while we *dissolve* in tears. Unless we *deep-six* whatever was needling us. We picture laughter *rippling around* a table, or a few words setting off a *froth* of excitement.

On our planet at least, living plants and animals need to ferry nutrients and send messages, and both require a benign liquid. Water is the great go-between. A medium fit to carry sediment or information or ships, it provides arteries for bodies and cities. We need water to assume new shapes, reorganize, change phase, assimilate, because each of our cells is a tiny saltwater lagoon with many harbors. When we enter the water, inserting our portable ocean into its, it feels snugly present, touching us all over, and we become pendant again, as we haven't been since the gestation of our last swim. But the body remembers the feel of floating in the womb, which may be why the sound of water is enough to lull.

Life is opportunistic, it adapts, it exploits what's available. So in one form or another, water greets us every day, from the liquid we splash on our faces to water locked inside the cells of nutritious heads of grain. We water our plants, our homes, our bodies. Our food is mainly water. And so water connects us to every other facet of life on earth, in one large flowing enterprise. Predator and prey share water holes, friend and foe share oases. Without water cultures founder, civilizations die. Does life exist elsewhere in the universe? Look for water. Water allows even unrelated substances to mix, tumble, and bark with electricity. Because water dissolves things, it's easy to pollute, and because water is persuadable, it's easy to rule. So protecting the planet's fresh water becomes an act of self-preservation. Though we can't always see downstream from reckless events, we pay dearly for that shortsightedness. Not if, but when. The web of life trembles on such fragile threads. Listen, now, in the distance, a calamity—can you hear it?—like thunder warnings before a summer storm.

A 130-pound woman is 65 pounds of plain water. But suppose I were entirely water? As water, I'd cascade and seep, soothe and corrode, serve as mirror or lens. I'd act as a traffic lane or a roadblock or a sacrament. I'd be invisible, odorless, colorless. Yet I'd batter the earth, I'd fall like andirons with large plunking raindrops, and blast away minute fragments of soil and rock, wearing down mountains, carving ice-cut valleys and frost-striped canyons. I'd stagger light. On rare occasions, as "diamond dust," I'd swirl and fall from air too cold for snow. In clouds, turning to crystal I'd fall; but in lakes and seas, turning to crystal I'd float. Because the soul of water is change, I'd dissolve almost anything on my travels through the ground and body, carrying sap and serum, minerals and blood, tiny chem labs to power thoughts and, at times, abominations. I'd sponge up the world around me, absorb new personas. And then, for a while at least, I'd strut out of the shadows, take the stage, and become visible, seasoned, a creature of substance with a real personality.

In portraits I'd look animal: two hydrogen atoms forming my ears, one plump oxygen atom my face. I'd live in bondage to hydrogen, that small common waif of an atom, and fat combustible oxygen. When hydrogen cozies up to oxygen, the magnetic attraction is so fierce it's hard to pry them apart. This would make me versatile, flexible, dynamic, with bonds continually breaking and reforging, as every puddle reacted as one electric whole, a fellowship that extended to entire oceans. I wouldn't swarm over surfaces as a thin film, but stick and stretch, clump and pile together, creating a dragnet that grips and carries things along.

Water, water everywhere. I'd be insistent, incessant, in torrents, in teacups, clinging to cool rocks, wobbling prisms of dew, supplying a bucket-brigade of bees with coolant for summer hives, shaping a baby's pudgy fingers. I'd ink the layout of cities, conduct traffic between empires, and incite border wars. I'd *reflect* so poignantly that humans would use the image to describe their mental world. I'd feed the rain-guzzling cottonwoods and willows, stiffen plant stems, pool belowground as a water table where life dines, and swirl on invisible winds across the sky. I'd bubble as saliva at the sight of a ripe apricot, ooze sweat during a dragon boat race, incubate life in womb-time. I'd incant poetry as I trickled over pebbles. I'd echo with whale song, crackle with fish talk, geyser up everywhere as life's wellspring, and herald the beginning and end of all thirst.

CRYSTALS

⟜

Dawn brings a gelatinous cold, where I dare not touch metal, breathing hurts deep in the bronchia, and I need a scarf around the neck to warm the air before it frosts my lungs. We're lucky that we can wear a climate and change it when we need to. The winter sun, riding low on the horizon, becomes a small piercing pupil in the center of a spectacular ice halo flanked by an obedient sun dog on either side. I don't know why the rainbow puddles are called sun dogs, except that they hound the sun. Someone dubbed them that in the 1700s and the name stuck. In the high atmosphere, tiny crystals form thin hexagonal tiles and six-sided columns, which fall toward Earth as ice prisms that split and reflect light, creating rainbow smears among the clouds or beside the sun. This morning, a spectral arc shines above the halo, and below it a brilliant sun pillar. The sky is dancing with tiny frozen crystals falling out of the blue.

On a walkabout, I find bottle-brush-shaped crystals which

have formed on small branches lying among the leaf clutter. But there's no frost on the ground and only certain twigs bear these frilly filamental crystals. They're tiny, which tilts my mind toward their opposite: the largest known crystals on Earth, buried in a silver and lead mine in Mexico. A thousand feet deep, miners discovered two caverns filled with row upon row of huge perfect selenite crystals—most about three feet wide and forty-five feet long. Selenite gets its name from the moon goddess Selene, and these immense crystals dazzle like light reflecting off a broken mirror. Fearing vandalism or theft, the mining company is keeping the whereabouts of the crystal caves a secret. The ambient temperature in the caves is deadly, anyway, an uninhabitable 150 degrees Fahrenheit with 100 percent humidity. Only by chance do we know about this hidden cave of the moon goddess. What other wonders lie beneath our feet?

Whether they're snow or selenite, crystals grow like cells, starting with a nub, then adding more, layer upon layer, duplicating, mobbing the way birds do around fallen fruit, with only a handful at first. Then the flock tightens into a crowd. Likewise, a small fragile snow crystal pulls water molecules from the air, forming more crystal around it. Seen through a microscope, the growing crystals look like tents or mountain ranges. Crystals wear many masks: ice, quartz, insulin, daffodil sap (the sharp crystals make it poisonous), meteorite, diamond, gypsum, fluorite, garnet (the largest on record weighs about 2,500 pounds), molten iron (which crystallizes as it cools). The mineral moolooite, a rare blue-green crystal discovered in 1986 at Mooloo Downs station in western Australia, forms when the guano from bats interacts with old copper sulfides! Electronics rely on crystal silicon and gallium arsenide. We clock our hours with vibrating quartz crystals, flavor our food with salt and sugar crystals. The gold carp in Japanese gardens shimmer their mirror-like crystals for camouflage when they feed near the surface. Some eye shadows' and shampoos' opal luster also comes from the amino acid guanine, which. when crystallized, twinkles with pearly light.

Some short-lived bacteria contain magnetic iron crystals that point toward true north and south; during their hour of life, magnetism draws them deeper into the soil. Viruses, arguably the most successful life-form on Earth, have crystal hearts, and, coincidentally, thrive in us, especially during the crystal fantasia of snow season. We used to assume the flu virus rampaged in winter because people stayed indoors, breathing the same air. But winter is flu paradise because the virus grows stable in cold dry air. staying aloft longer and drifting farther, suspended in droplets like hot-air balloons. Cool air travels well into our lungs with flu viruses aboard, ready to lodge. In summer, weighed down by hot humid weather, the flu virus grows soggy and falls to the ground. But in winter it spreads better on the way to the subway than in a warm room. And thanks to air travel, people can act as hatcheries, carrying flu with them even in the off season. Honeybees also carry magnetic crystals in their abdomens to help them navigate. Cows probably do, too, because when they're grazing in a field, they tend to face magnetic north. Do we?

Like bees, the Vikings used crystals to navigate, but they worked a different property of crystals. According to Viking sagas, on overcast days or during the long season of winter twilight, the navigators held aloft and rotated "sunstones" to locate the whereabouts of the sun. None of the mysterious objects have been discovered, but there are several candidates, including cordierite, a crystal common on Scandinavian coasts, and Icelandic spar (optical calcite). Using crystals as a sun compass that changed from blue to light yellow when pointed at the sun, the Vikings learned to interpret sky patterns well enough to navigate in fog and clouds. In an ancient Icelandic saga one finds: "The weather was thick and stormy. . . . The king looked about and saw no blue sky. . . . Then the king took the sunstone and held it up, and then he saw where the Sun beamed from the stone." An updated version of the sunstone, the military's "sky compass," relies on man-made polarizing filters.

The ancient Egyptians used crushed crystals in medicines, and also in singing crystal bowls to rekindle harmony between the physical and spiritual worlds. At a spa several years ago, I sat with a healer who played an opaque white crystal bowl somewhat like a glass harmonica. When he struck it with a rubber mallet the bowl gave a resounding gong, as of a distant clock tower, and as he moved the mallet around the rim, the bowl chanted different sounds depending on where he placed his free hand. The gongs grew in resonance and tone, the vibrations washed through my body, and after a few minutes the singing felt so loud I couldn't hear any speaking and my body vibrated inside, playing a thickly present note. Since flesh is mainly water, the sound rippled right through it, hitting the bones and cartilage, which resonated in harmony, creating a sound massage.

ONE BAD ROOSTER SPOILS
THE BARNYARD

There was a child went forth every day,
And the first object he look'd upon,
that object he became,
And that object became part of him
for the day or a certain part of the day,
Or for many years or stretching cycles of years.

—WALT WHITMAN

WE'RE SOMETIMES SERENADED BY roosters at dawn,
except that today they've gone off too early in mine-
shaft darkness. You'd think a consensus of roosters would out-
vote a lone bird who's lost his internal clock, but according
to the farmers it works the other way. One rooster can spoil a
whole barnyard. Like a persuasive juror who sways all the others, an offbeat rooster whose circadian rhythms were scrambled
by living in a barn under artificial light can incite a barnyard to
crow on a new schedule. It doesn't take much to prompt a riot
of early crowing. Far up the lake, beyond the yacht club, nature
center, and Boy Scout summer camp, one farmer raises roosters
for their red combs—the key ingredient in the wildly popular
injections marketed to boomers with bad knees. Cockscomb is

a rich source of the sugar molecule *hyaluronan*, used in Synvisc and Hyalgan, injectible lubricants for arthritic joints.

I'm lucky to live in a town of seven gorges, two colleges, small-town neighborhoods, but also many farmers, some of them devoutly organic. Stick and Stone Farm is owned by my friends Lucy and Chaw and their one-year-old Greta, whose middle name in Chinese means "iridescent sheen around the moon." Pausing beside the farm still in darkness on this Saturday morning, it's wonderful to watch dawn percolating among the vegetables.

This is a season of pumpkins, squash, and root vegetables, and Stick and Stone is known for all of those, including several varieties of heirloom beets. *Borscht*, beet soup, was often on the menu while I was growing up. Slavic cuisine revolves around beets, with beets also used medicinally for sore throats and colds—beet broth, vinegar, and honey for a gargle, sage and beet juice to calm sore throats, warm beet juice dropped into the ear to ease tinnitus, and a poultice of beet leaves applied to the brow for headaches. My great-grandparents would have grown beets, and used them medicinally, on their small farm in southern Poland. And when they were Greta's age? I bet they were just as enchanted with the oddly shaped vegetables.

After all, these organic beets lie on the gravel path like round-bellied dolls. Oddly curved necks give the squash poses too animal to ignore—the cocked eye of disbelief, the tilted head of bafflement. And there are times when radishes can gaze up at one with huge feline longing. Nature, in such moods at least, can look happy, as it does on the fixed smile of dolphins (just an anatomical illusion). As children, we automatically respond to any hint of a face. Only later might we wonder about the notion of vegetable personality, loath to quite surrender it, yet aware of maybe looking foolish. The mind has its underground, its captives and secrets that, if revealed, would result in ridicule or, worse yet, *strangeness*, that living death.

A shovel leaning against a fence hints at a story. The early-morning light shines whitely down the spine of the blade, which exists as a clear message: a human was working hard here. Who was the person who paused, arranged the shovel so that it wouldn't fall, and walked away to do something else perhaps, and forgot where he had left it? Or was it left there on purpose as a reminder, like plowing only half of one sentence of soil? It is the symbol of work: a perfectly designed callipygous blade and long wooden handle the right bore for gripping. Dawn chores include turning the free-range chickens loose and checking for fresh eggs. digging irrigation ditches, harvesting and washing the kale, corn, and root vegetables and preparing them for restaurants, grocers, and markets. Many a morning, Chaw plows the acreage on an old tractor, with baby Greta in his arms, as the moon floats above in its iridescent sheen. When she grows up, will she remember these bouncy tractor rides with dad as farmwork or child's play? Her playroom stretches from horizon to horizon, and she crawls on all fours like some of her woolly playmates.

Back at home, my neighbors Georg and Lucia encourage their kids to play outdoors, and I often see the family climbing among the branches of an old red maple in their front yard, building a dozen bluebird houses, or sliding around ecstatically in the snow. I think that's unusual for kids in these days of PlayStations, MySpace, and instant messaging.

Children have always played in the landscapes of the mind, the inscapes of the indoors and outscapes of the outdoors, sometimes imagining the outdoors while playing indoors. We play, having no alternative, thanks to the wannabe spirit of evolution, alive in our cells from birth onward, grooming us, maybe until our last out-breath, to best yet another monster or hardship. Play we must, to learn, love, grow, survive, even if it wasn't fun or required, both of which in the finest, feathered sense it is.

But for ages, children played in nature, because there was no indoors on the veldt, or the indoors (tent, lodge, cave) was cramped, or, more importantly, because they didn't distinguish themselves from nature. They played at being something else, someone else, the not-me in sheep's clothes, the half-sheep, the whole *baah*-full quadrupedal sheep itself. I'm sure they played at being insentient things, too, mountains and water, moon and trees.

A wooden Radio Flyer sled still skates through the ante-rooms of my memory, along with a stuffed elephant, the taste of icicle melt on the tongue, and the sound of water plashing over pebbles. I've never stopped playing in nature, our ultimate and only mother and tutor. For instance, after heavy snowfalls, I like to walk down the street shaking hands with the snow-topped arms of evergreens, one after another, as if they were part of some long receiving line. Shaking limbs jars loose the snow on higher branches, with the sudden release of a soft avalanche down the length of my body.

I was a little kid in the futuristic jet-propelled fifties, basking in the novelty of black-and-white television, Bakelite phones, and instant cake mix, but minus computers, iPods, and such. We played indoors, but we also begged, whined big-time: *Can I go outside and play?* For many reasons, among them safety and marketing, kids today play increasingly indoors, solo, with some avatar of electronics. Now that toy shops offer a pint-sized

ATM machine, you know you've skipped right over the Land of Oz childhood and splashed down in a regatta of moth-proof, skin-the-shin-proof games that improve skills like hand-eye coordination, but nix the hard-earned gift of attending to life at length, in momentous moments, not just in attention blinks. As a fourth grader in San Diego told Richard Louv, who coined the term "nature-deficit disorder": "I like to play indoors 'cause that's where all the electrical outlets are."

What becomes of children when they don't play outside, watching the sun move across the sky, squirreling around in trees, pocketing daddy longlegs, poking a hand into frog spawn? Nature presses on us always and from all sides, including the nickel-hearted earth arcing energy beneath our feet. Nature sculpts and calms us, hones and homesteads us, whether we're aware of it or not, and when children are parted from nature for too long, their compass floats and they can lose their own wilderness, the adder wildness of being one animal among many fascinating others, in an action-packed green world, whose single lesson is *change*.

Vaya is the Hindu god of the winds, who represents the healing breath of change. In Sacramento, psychiatrist Dr. Claude Arnett runs the Vaya Mental Health practice, which specializes in children and young adults with serious mental and addictive ills, and where nature play figures importantly in any therapy. Nature-deficit disorder, he feels, gravely affects the nervous systems of today's children and their ability to handle stress. The sympathetic ("flight or fight") part of the nervous system focuses on details, analyzing them for danger, and it engages quickly to solve a problem or perform a task. In contrast, the parasympathetic system regards a wider field of view, with senses open, lazily taking in the whole world. First we scan the landscape, then we target something specific, perhaps focus on a moving beetle. Nature play teaches children to move fluidly between the two skills, alternating field focus and target focus, the one and the many, dove and wheeling flock. Television and video games only teach the first, a target-oriented form of attention. Arnett finds that when troubled children spend time in nature their mental world brightens, they develop greater elasticity and come to him more flexible and adaptive. Even lifelong city dwellers, given images to rank, put wilderness photographs at the top, and number one among those is a scene of the African grasslands. How could it be otherwise? We evolved on the savannas, and in the deepest furrows of our humanity we remember that sun-drenched world. A ten-year study of surgery patients found that people recovering in rooms with a view of a grove of trees (as opposed to office buildings) had lower stress levels and went home days sooner.

On the short-lived hoary visitors we call shooting stars, I wish for many planet-clad dawns as luminous as this one. And in the spirit of Celtic blessings, I add: May our cities be redesigned to include more trees and windows, providing a greater sense of sunrise, sunset, and seasons. May playing in nature not be regarded as idle; may our health plans cover green holidays to parks and wildernesses as some Scandinavian plans already do. May our schools teach us to marvel at our humble origins in the minute stuff of the cosmos, and the fascinating life-forms we have nonetheless become. May many people have the opportunity to behold the planet from space and return with a fuller sense of what *home* means. At least once, may madcap roosters serenade us at dawn.

AFTER HOURS

✦

FOR ME, DAWN BEGINS BEFORE sunrise and extends up through sky and weather to the canopy of stars. The visible stars, that is. So much surrounds us that we can't see. Life on other planets, but also the missing matter in the universe. Computations show that stars, planets, galaxies, and all the rest of the visible matter make up only 4 percent of what actually exists. Where is the rest, the so-called "dark matter" and even stranger "dark energy"? A yard or street is partly full of the invisible weight of the universe.

At the doorway of the senses, the self chances upon the world. Yet for the most part, we live a life of surfaces; otherwise we'd buckle under an avalanche of sensations. When we turn on the radio in the morning and hear "static" or "interference" as we switch between channels, do we need to know we're divining lightning strikes on other continents and the hissing death throes of galaxies? Probably not. But when we do, the aperture of the mind widens as it travels to distant continents and galaxies and back again.

After the black dawn, the white dawn arrives laced with pink fire. Dawn light brings a clarity that's missing from noon glare or smoggy sunset, however pretty their filters. Sitting on a rusty wrought-iron chair, I turn my thoughts to the beauty of rust, which dissects metal so meticulously, creating free-form bronzes, brown bubbling sandwiches, gritty red icons, supine statuettes, ragged perforations, flaking black-orange memorials to time. We underestimate rust, which may well have sponsored all of life on Earth. In the explicit light, rust declares its past.

Some think it's easy for life to emerge, for primitive cells like bacteria to form anywhere in the universe. For instance, in the deep-ocean trenches, several miles below the sunlit waves, hyperthermophiles bloom—hardy bacteria that breathe iron and thrive in water hot enough to sterilize surgery tools. Hugging the scalding vents, they reproduce in boiling water and can abide at 266 degrees Fahrenheit where minerals abound. One of the many heat-loving microbes haunting the deep ocean, *Geobacter metallireducens* can even generate its own electricity.

All you really need is rocks and water, and everything else happens by itself. When iron sulfide (rust) from Earth's hot core meets cold water, the shock creates honeycombed chimneys where the first living cells could have grown. Subject oxygen and carbon dioxide—so plentiful on the young Earth—to heat and high pressure, with rust as a catalyst, and a metabolism naturally ensues. The earliest microbes would have left those cradles to colonize the land. We still carry some of that primordial iron in our cells today. Rust is a very slow fire, and like fire it releases energy as it devours. It also gains in size, prying apart steel in a process known as "iron smacking." Iron corrodes especially fast when exposed to an electrolyte like water, and, for better and worse, the human body is awash with an electrolyte broth.

Rust, I bow to you, I say silently, not wanting to disturb the birds that have begun to pipe, trill, and bark, chasing each other at speed across the sky. My rusty, weathered chair is rich with the fetching poverty the Japanese call *wabi sabi.*

Wabi originally meant living miserably alone in nature, far from human society, and feeling gloomy, bleak, comfortless. And *sabi,* whose beauty comes from the patina of age, originally meant "chill," "lean," "withered." But the phrase *wabi sabi* changed in the sixteenth century, when the hermit's life of chosen isolation in the woods seemed to offer a spiritual richness society lacked, and the words came to mean an intimacy with nature and delight in the rustic details of daily life. The hermit's eye turned toward the minute, the crude, the cracked, the incomplete, those objects with interesting crevices—especially if something was rusted, weathered, or worn, revealing the passage of time. It's a nice felicity that the Japanese word for rust, 錆, is also pronounced *sabi,* returning us once more to the rusty origins of life and the rust at the heart of the word "rustic." Partly as a rebellion against the glory of the decorative arts, *wabi sabi* favored the purity of humble forms, but unlike European modernism's ideal of smooth, streamlined, futuristic creations, *wabi sabi* valued the organic, imperfect, faded nature of earthy things that were handmade one at a time, not mass-produced, and all the more appealing when worn through loving use. *Wabi sabi* relies on intuitive, right-here right-now observation, without any glance toward the future or even the idea of progress.

A pastoral aesthetic, *wabi sabi* not only accepts nature as unruly and uncontrollable, it welcomes nature's rule, beyond the scope of any technology we can create, however sleek and obedient. So *wabi sabi* embraces the idea of corrosion, decay to the point of disintegration, and ambiguity, in warm fluid shapes and quietly resonating earth tones. Poetry, too, can be *wabi sabi* if it arouses serene melancholy, an acceptance of reality at its most exquisitely mundane, a reality in which things and people break down, but are no less beautiful for that.

Japanese also has many names for beauty. One feels *awaré* while appreciating the ephemeral, say the transient beauty of decay in the luminous green moss spreading over rotting trees, the mushrooms and toadstools rising from the rich soil, the patches of brilliant gold and red lichen. After a bird has flown, one may feel *yoin*, silent reverberations that remain. It's this sensation that poet Wallace Stevens writes of in "Thirteen Ways of Looking at a Blackbird," when he celebrates both "The blackbird whistling / Or just after." One may also experience the poignant beauty known as *yūgen*, described in this way by thirteenth-century author Kamo no Chōmei (in *An Account of my Hut*, 1212): "It is like an autumn evening under a colorless expanse of silent sky. Somehow, as if for some reason that we should be able to recall, tears well uncontrollably." Or: "When looking at autumn mountains through mist, the view may be indistinct yet have great depth. Although few autumn leaves may be visible through the mist, the view is alluring. The limitless vista created in imagination far surpasses anything one can see more clearly."

Solar energy lights our days and fuels the plants prey animals eat before they're eaten by predators. We eat the sunshine stored in those plants and animals, burning it for energy which we spend to work, cook, make love, play music, pursue games. And so we're connected to every other life-form on Earth in a skein of interrelated victories of fire, including rust. The universe is most likely littered with planets as rusty as our own. Are they florid with life? If so, how well, and how long, have their life-forms survived?

That question almost qualifies as a koan. Koans are capsules of thought, psychic knots that resist unraveling. In some Buddhist sects, students are assigned phrases or situations to meditate upon, to focus the mind and free it from the bear trap of reason. For example:

1. A man is sitting atop a hundred-foot pole. How does he get off it?
2. A wheel maker makes two wheels, each with fifty spokes. Suppose you cut out the hubs. Would there still be wheels?
3. On a windy day, two monks are arguing about a fluttering banner. The first says, "The banner is moving, not the wind." The second says, "The wind is moving, not the banner." Who is right?
4. Two hands clap and there is a sound; what is the sound of one hand?
5. What is the straight within the bent?
6. Pull a five-story pagoda out of a teapot.

Inexhaustible, koans are intended for live practice between master and student, with illumination as a goal, not interpretation, because, as an old saying goes, "it's easy to confuse the pointing finger with the moon." As Zen teacher Norman Fischer explains: "This practice consists of living with and sitting with phrases, until they become very large and very strange, and reveal themselves to us. That is to say, through them we are revealed to ourselves." There's no right answer to these puzzles designed to focus the mind, and I sometimes dwell on koans while waiting in the dark for first light. This morning, I've been thinking a little about *mu*, though I appreciate it's not something understood by occasional thought. *Mu*, which translates inadequately as "nothingness," often appears in Buddhist practice, and sometimes in this venerable koan: "What is *mu?*"

As I sit under a coliseum of stars awaiting the dawn, *mu* is the everythingness of everything fed by and in time with the everythingness of everything else, except that its particles are too small to be captured in the net of words like "every" or "thing" or "net," which, like life-forms and galaxies, are only temporary clumps of the stridently irrational *mu*, a mutable, ultimately manic, mute, munificent force that strings us together as it does the farthest stars. And I am only using the unwieldy image of "force" because we are the sort of beings who do, to communicate the shred of universe we homestead and can perceive, when of course there is no force, no we, no universe, not even *mu*-mesons, only these molecules, this energy pooling here for a short while as diane, and never again in the same way.

I once read of a Zen master who became enlightened like this: "When I heard the temple bell ring, suddenly there was no bell and no I, just sound." Imagine no distinction between yourself and the bell, the sound and the universe. Sometimes when I'm swimming, the waves don't feel separate, the water's history and my history melt together and I sense my particles breaking apart and scattering, returning now and then like a school of fish to form what appears solid, pattern, thing, but happens only to be a temporary sack of cells turning together. As sunlight hits the prismatic water, the walls and floor of the pool become a luminous cage holding nothing but thought. Ever since I was a child, for whole minutes at a time, I have effervesced out of my self in an ecstasy of communion with the cosmos at the level of atom and leaf. And yet, I also spend most of each day not in that state, with my zaftig "I" sprawling all over the mind furniture. a slovenly and selfish guest. So is enlightenment sustainable? Jack Kornfield, a founding teacher at the Spirit Rock Center in Woodacre, California, explains that enlightenment isn't continuous, one still has to do the laundry. But surely *how* one does the laundry is what matters? Fine, but one still has to go to work, not always with equanimity. Unless one lives in a monastery, it's not easy to prolong a calm, serene, cheerful equilibrium, which one nerve-jangling phone call can quickly convert to anxiety. In the stir of the world, I'm glad to find slender moments of dawning, when the ephemeral cape of being simply fits.

In the end, life is the best koan—not the word, but the process of living. An endlessly mutating koan created by water, minerals, and heat in the cold furnace of the atom, without meaning or purpose. From that evolved creatures stricken by meaning, afflicted with purpose. But it has always been about rust, the ancient, unknowable, nearly unthinkable rust that created all life, and the rust that obliterates us, intimately, one by one.

THE SILENCE THAT IS NOT THERE
AND THE SILENCE THAT IS

⌒

WINTER TREES BRING TO MIND Eastern gods, whose many limbs curve gracefully, touching the universe in all directions. When the wind rocks their branches, a few last marcescent leaves whisper eerily. The world brims with foreign languages, spoken much as we speak—by passing air over solid forms whose various holes and flexings fine-tune the sounds. It doesn't matter whose or what's breath is used, or sometimes what liquid, since sound travels so well through water. The great Lake Cayuga, deep and soupy with life in late summer, and shaped by millennia of erosion and sediment, has its own key, and waterfowl and frogs float their calls on the water. Sounds carry over frozen water, too—in the Arctic, voices can travel for a mile across hard flat snow.

A friend has invited me on a silent retreat. Relatively silent. After all, the birds would still sing and call, the leaves rustle, the cicadas scrape, the wind sough. Exclude them, leave the galaxy even, and there's still the background hiss from the Big

Bang which radio telescopes record as a sort of hoarse streaming sigh. I mean human silence, which on this retreat also
includes turning off the wordless communications, what the
Japanese call *haragei* (pronounced ha-ra-GAY), body language,
gesture, facial expression, a telling glance.

"Soon silence will have passed into legend," sculptor Jean
Arp warns in *Sacred Silence*. "Man has turned his back on
silence. Day after day he invents machines and devices that
increase noise and distract humanity from the essence of life,
contemplation, meditation. Tooting, howling, screeching,
booming, crashing, whistling, grinding, and trilling bolster
his ego."

Once a year, on a changing day in April, people in Bali
celebrate Nyepi (pronounced nn-YEH-pee), a national day of
silence that follows the dark moon of the spring equinox and
ushers in the Balinese New Year. On this Hindu holiday, both
car and foot traffic are prohibited (except for emergency vehicles), radio and TV must play low if at all; village wardens keep
people off the beaches; work, socializing, and even lovemaking
stops, as a nation sits and falls silent together, for one day of
introspection in an otherwise hectic year. Not only does the
dawn sound different, it smells different. Without the reeking
exhaust from cars and trucks masking subtler scents, the air
smells naturally floral, and it's enriched by the green aromas
of vine-clad forests.

During Nyepi, surrounded by the incense of wildflowers,
one mulls over values, beholds the balance of nature, medi-
tates on love, compassion, kindness, patience. Dogs bark, cicadas call shrilly, but the streets breathe a quiet rare for that
clamorous island, a silence framed like a painting. Not the
silence of deep space, nor the hush of a dark room, but an

achieved silence, a found silence that's refined and full. The Japanese word for silence, *mokurai*, combines *moku*, silence, with *rai*, thunder, creating a sense of silence as a powerful force, a reverse thunder. One doesn't *fall* silent when tasting impermanence—the sting of everything appearing, disappearing, and changing from moment to moment—but undergoes silence, creates silence, becomes silence.

There are many forms of silence: the silence after raindrops fall on the metal roof of an old corn binder pickup truck, the silence just before the word *silence*, and just after, the silence of light cutting through the pool water to stencil giraffe hide onto the bottom, the silence that exists when your dead mother no longer calls your name, the silence inside manicotti-shaped sleeping bags when the sleepers have left, the silence of one's DNA when one is scattered dust, the silence of neurons sparkling in the lens of a scanning electron microscope, the silence inside the ear when a phone call ends, the silence thick with the silences of loved ones, the silence of other paths one might have taken, the silence of recluse firmaments glimpsed through a telescope, the silence between one's hands cupped in prayer, the silence that water striders leave in their wake, the silence of a yolk-yellow sun running atop the horizon at dawn, the silence that we package into seconds and minutes, the minute silence of all packages, the silence of the crying baby one never had, the silence of swimming in thick furry ocean, the silence of snow pressed against one's closed eyelids, the silence that hung in the air after you said: "Will you write those thoughts down?" when what you really meant was "Will you write those down *for me*?," the silence of the fog left by one's breath on a chilly morning, the silence of your name before you were born, the silence of slow-motion memories, the silence of quaking

aspen leaves viewed through a window, the silence of wandering thistledown, the silence of igneous rock, the silence of
mirrors, the silence held by the *b* in the word *doubt*, the infinite silence reflected in all silences, the silence of an inactive
volcano, the silence of the heart's stilled motor.

Death is the silence in an invisible valise carried under
one arm. As we walk, an elbow leaves room for it. Through a
window I see quaking aspens fidgeting silently (the glass baffles
noise) in a dumb show of shivering leaves. Surely my death will
dawn like that: first the aspens will flicker; then the scene will
fade to black and white; leaves will spin even faster in the wind,
but silently, and I will have been.

TIME WELL SPENT

If the only prayer you said in your whole life was
"thank you," that would be enough.

—MEISTER ECKHART

SO MANY MARVELS ARE BUSTLING through this slender
dawn: Lens-shaped clouds signaling high winds aloft. Roof
shingles overlapping like dove feathers. A busily sniffing dog
reading its scent-version of the morning newspaper. On tree
limbs and window ledges, birds facing upwind, to keep their
feathers ironed shut, not ruffled up by the breeze. And several
apes, walking down the street on their way to work, engaging
in social pantomime. Such is the texture of life, the *feel* of
being alive on this particular planet.

Most evenings, I think about the day's experiences, and
choose one that stands out. It may be as zesty as a bowl of
great lemon sorbet, as eye-opening as a passage in a book,
as peaceful as a lunchtime snooze, as unexpected as a quick
slant of sunlight catching dust particles in the air, as pulse-
revving as a long-awaited letter, or as smoldery smooth as a
piece of Endangered Species 70 percent cacao dark chocolate.
Or maybe realizing for the first time that the blue butterfly on

its wrapper is a Karner blue, named years ago by fellow Ithacan Vladimir Nabokov, and that the last remaining Karner blues now live among the whooping cranes in Necedah National Wildlife Refuge. An odd synchronicity. Embellishing that realization with words helps to store it in memory. What was the best thing that happened? Reviewing the day's delights often yields surprises, and serves as a reminder of how full a life is, how lucky some days feel, and how even stressful days may contain glowing nuggets of peace, pleasure, or joy.

We can't enchant the world, which makes its own magic; but we can enchant ourselves by paying deep attention. My life has been changing, I've been near death several times, experienced the illness and death of loved ones, and the simple details of being have become precious. But I also relish life's sensory festival and the depot where nature and human nature meet. Everything that happens to us—from choosing the day's shoes to warfare—shines at that crossroads.

To reflect the instantaneous takes time, and Monet achieved it through a sort of reverse weathering, like the buildup of crystals. In increments barely visible to the naked eye, he layered one brushstroke upon the other, sometimes just skipping a dry brush across the surface to create a flickering quality. Other times, he mixed colors right on the canvas so that you can see the pigments meeting and blending. Or he painted in corrugations— heavy brushstrokes applied perpendicular, touching only the ridges of the thinner layer underneath.

"Fat over thin" is basic to oil painting, and for a painting to dry properly, each layer should be thicker than the one below it, layer upon layer, and progressively oilier, or it risks cracking. Unlike thinner fluids, oil paints don't evaporate as they dry but oxidize—they rust!—which can take months or years. Many art conservators regard an oil painting as truly dry only after eighty years. So although he painted instants, it took them nearly a century to solidify. For years after Monet finished a painting, even while viewers admired it, the pigments were still in motion, changing invisibly before their eyes.

In his eighties, with failing eyesight, he once more painted the steeply arched Japanese footbridge in his garden. This time he painted it in thick autumnal colors—brown, red, gold, orange, and green streaks—with only the merest suggestion of a bridge, its railing slabs of blue, the sun vertical brushstrokes of ochre and white shining through the open panels. It doesn't give the impression of a mist-clad morning softening the edges of things and veiling summer's shrieking greens and florals. Instead it's an abstraction seen by a deteriorating eye, in jagged edges, angles of paint and heavy strokes of color declaring their relationship to one another, their strings to the world, their reflection of the rising sun, and their debt to Monet's aging grip on the instantaneous.

It's as if he were reaching a brush-wielding hand back onstage from the wings, waving to an audience whose rough whereabouts and clothes he remembers. A Monet still animated, creative, and alive, but declining, not fading but its opposite—becoming heavier-handed and more abstract. Even with most of its details gone, his world still existed as changing instants of color. "I only see blue," he complained to a doctor at Giverny in June 1924. "I no longer see red . . . or yellow. I know these colors exist because I know that on my palette there is red, yellow, a special green, a certain violet; I no longer see them as I once did, and yet I remember very well the colors which they gave me." His sunrises from this period look dark to us, and they did to him, too, but only after several operations to have cataracts removed. Then he looked at his recent paintings, dismayed by all the brown, and destroyed some. When the cataract scales fell from his eyes and he saw the world restored, he repainted some of the water lilies, making them brighter than before. To his friend and art dealer Paul Durand-Ruel, he once wrote: "Everything is pigeon-throated and punch ablaze. It's wonderful."

As Monet chronicled, no time is more alive than the intimate now, where truths are eternal. Our sense of time changes as we grow, from the elongated days of childhood to the quickening years of old age. We pass through different time zones. Children digest more information, and faster, than adults, and since everything is new, and much of it flashy, there's a bundle to process and it seems to go slowly. The elderly sense the world with a slower metabolism, and they find fewer surprises, so life seems to stream by. Increase anyone's metabolism—with a shock for instance, and adrenaline pours to handle the emergency. Then the brain speeds through information, since any detail may count. Time slows down. This is also the world of predator and prey. It's odd picturing other animals existing in their own private time zones, but I think they must. More than anything else, what we pay attention to helps define us.

With what do we choose to spend the irreplaceable hours of our life? That question comes painfully and late to some, to many only on their deathbeds, and to others, like me, repeatedly and deniably over the years (especially so if one is raising a family), and then repeatedly but less deniably. How one soothes oneself then takes different forms. Myself, I have been a restless sleeper, waking often through this dream, then plunging back into a death-denying sleep. With the death of parents, the looming death of a spouse, the death of younger friends, it's hard to sleep quite as soundly. I wake, and when I do the beauty of the world, however fleeting, fills me with an incontestable joy that leaches right into my bloodstream. I need only allow it in. Born into a world of light, my senses mature and will decay. But until they do they are the gateways to the mysterious kingdom in which I find myself, one I could not have imagined, a land not entirely of hope and glory, yet no less beautiful for that.

We exist as phantom, monster, miracle, each a theme park all one's own, and mainly unknowable in the end, not just to others, but to ourselves as well. I often think about the charade of trying to capture a self in a mirror. One day we feel like the toast of the town, the next day the hoax, one moment flighty, the next fully present for and part of life's contrapuntal fugue. Think about the lunacy of the Moon landing, the lunatic fringe of wild loons on a lake in the Aleutians. A word is a kind of pebble in the hand, at once irritant, worry bead, reminder. Nothing surpasses the single suchness of this moment. Presence is always a present, a gift, intransitively given, in some stage of unwrap, waiting to be explored.

Just show up. That's all we have to do, that's all I do when I am fully present, for good or bad, right here, right now, without thinking about work or recess. A sleeper can wake and be lured out of bed by the sorcery of the sky as day is dawning. Time well spent. After all (or more accurately, during all), I may not live to the end of this sentence, to lift my felt-tipped pen and settle a tiny black dot on the page. I did. But that was then and this is now, the thisness of what is, the ripening dawn.

ACKNOWLEDGMENTS

HEARTFUL THANKS TO DAVA SOBEL, for casting her eagle eye over an early draft of *Dawn Light*, and fairygodmother thanks to Zoe, just for being herself. A lexicon of thanks to Alane Mason, my patient and savvy editor. Charmed thanks to Suzanne Gluck, my agent extraordinaire. Detailed thanks to Liz Butler, literary assistant and wombat wrangler. Sisterly thanks to Dan, OJohn, and Jon. Restorative thanks to Dr. Ann. Multifaceted thanks to Philip. And tender, connubial thanks to Paul.